THE GOLF COURSES OF
JACK NICKLAUS

THE GOLF COURSES OF
JACK NICKLAUS

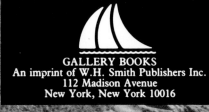

GALLERY BOOKS
An imprint of W.H. Smith Publishers Inc.
112 Madison Avenue
New York, New York 10016

Published by Gallery Books
A Division of WH Smith Publishers Inc
112 Madison Avenue
New York, New York 10016

Produced by
Brompton Books Corp
15 Sherwood Place
Greenwich, CT 06830

ISBN 0-8317-3920-7

Printed in Hong Kong

10 9 8 7 6 5 4 3 2 1

Designed by Tom Debolski
Edited and written by Timothy Jacobs

Editor's note:
Unless otherwise indicated, distances are in yards. This is
true of the Nicklaus courses in Canada, Japan, the United
Kingdom and in the United States.

This book was produced by American Graphic Systems
of San Francisco, California, a firm not associated with
Jack Nicklaus Golf Services or any other entity or enter-
prise of Jack Nicklaus.

Page 1: **The eighteenth green at Valhalla Golf Club, a
new Jack Nicklaus design in Kentucky. The forked
fairway trails down the side of the creek at right; its
secondary prong is visible at photo left.**
Pages 2–3: **A view from the eighth green at
Breckenridge Golf Club. Breckenridge is situated
amidst the spectacular scenery of the Colorado Rocky
Mountains.**
These pages: **The third green at the Australian Golf
Club, a historic facility, newly reworked by Jack
Nicklaus. The Australian is located just a few miles
southwest of Sydney, in 'the Land Down Under.'**

TABLE OF CONTENTS

Introduction:
Jack Nicklaus' Golden Touch

Jack Nicklaus

I magine being faced with the perfect challenge—one that takes place in an environment of exquisite natural beauty; a challenge that is tailored to test your abilities, and presents, at various intervals, the chance to do something really extraordinary. If you have ever played on a Jack Nicklaus golf course, then you have found that challenge. Each course is a unique experience that combines extraordinary aesthetics with a versatility of design that will present itself afresh to you time after time.

This book is a guided tour of the world of Jack Nicklaus golf course design. While some courses could not be presented here for various reasons, we believe that we have assembled an interesting selection that will serve to exemplify the stimulating variety, and the development, of Jack Nicklaus' design concepts. Here too, you the reader may get a sense of the ongoing desire and dedication with which Mr Nicklaus and his associates are committed to the advancement of golf by the building of exceptional courses.

There is ample evidence to justify *Golf Digest*'s statement that 'His courses are noted for being first-class in every respect.' Jack Nicklaus has designed or co-designed some of the greatest golf courses in the world, and has been involved in the design or redesign of almost 90 courses to date. With accolades pouring in from everywhere, there is a sense of understatement in the quote—from former PGA president Joe Black (in a publicity release from Nicklaus' spectacular new Desert Mountain complex in Arizona)—that 'Jack Nicklaus is acknowledged to be in the forefront of golf course designers in America.'

While it would seem reasonable to begin a book about his golf course designs with a startling revelation about one or all of them, we can at this point only enhance our

readers' appreciation of the artistry and intelligence that is the source of these designs—for few are ignorant of the fact that Jack Nicklaus, lauded as one of America's great course designers, and by many as the greatest *player* of the game of golf *ever*, is also one of the *world's* finest golf course designers. We'll have more on this, later, for the above claims could quite rightly be called extravagant boasts if not for the fact that objective criteria declare them to be accurate, and further, such praise comes not from Jack Nicklaus himself. It is but part of the overwhelming approval heaped upon him as a golfer, a course designer, a family man and an all-around human being. If ever a man had the Midas touch—without the negatives mythically attributed to such—then Jack Nicklaus certainly has it.

Of course, to consider the work of any artist, one has to consider the wellsprings of that art—the artist's life, what he has done with it, and what his influences have been. Jack William Nicklaus was born in Columbus, Ohio on 21 January 1940, the son of

Louis Charles (Junior) and Helen N Nicklaus. The younger Nicklaus began taking golfing lessons at the age of 10, at Donald Ross' superb Scioto Country Club (reworked by D Wilson in 1963), near his boyhood home in the Columbus suburb of Upper Arlington. His teacher then—and in fact the only formal teacher he's ever had—was Jack Grout, who has, throughout the years, helped Nicklaus to stay on his game.

A brilliant golfer, Mr Nicklaus also possesses a high degree of acumen and coordination for sports in general—in junior high school in Upper Arlington, he was the quarterback, punter and placekicker on the football team; the center on the basketball team; the catcher on the baseball team; and an 11-second 100-yard dash sprinter on the track team. In high school, he gave up baseball and football for basketball. He switched from center to forward, and as a junior and senior, he was named to the all-league team in the Central Buckeye League.

At Ohio State University, where he studied from 1957–62, Jack focused on golf, which, as we know, was to become his life's vocation. He has, however, never lost his delight in engaging in other sports as a hobby. Jack Nicklaus, his wife and children have always had a very close family life that centers on playing sports together.

Jack himself is a life-long devoted fisherman, loves to play tennis (and has two grass courts at his home in North Palm Beach, Florida), still loves to shoot baskets at the hoop mounted over the garage of his home, likes swimming in the family pool, enjoys throwing and kicking the football (he's quite good at both) and his latest-blooming sports passion is skiing—which, over the last decade, has been *the* family sport for the Nicklaus clan.

Since this present volume deals with the golf courses that Mr Nicklaus has designed,

we can present only a brief outline of his astonishing accomplishments as a *player on golf courses*. His record of 20 major championship victories is an astonishment in itself, as the great Bobby Jones had previously set the record at 13, and this number of major championship victories was considered to be beyond the reach of other mortals until Jack Nicklaus proved that reasonable assumption to be in error.

At last count, he had won 89 tournament victories worldwide, including the following major tournaments—the US Amateur, 1959 and 1961; the Tournament of Champions, 1963, 1964, 1971, 1973 and 1977; the US Open, 1962, 1967, 1972 and 1980; the US Masters, 1963, 1965, 1966, 1972 and 1975; the British Open, 1966, 1970 and 1978; the PGA Championship, 1963, 1971, 1973, 1974 and 1980; the International Pro-Amateur, 1973; the Atlanta Golf Classic 1973; the Walt Disney Golf Classic, 1973; the Hawaiian Open, 1974; the Tournament Players Championship, 1974; the Tournament Players Championship (Hawaii) 1975; the Doral-Eastern Open, the Heritage Classic, the Masters, the PGA Championship, the World Open, 1976; the Australian Open, 1964, 1968, 1971, 1975,

1976 and 1978; the World Series of Golf, 1977; the Gleason Inverrary Classic, 1977; the Philadelphia Classic, 1978; the Colonial National Invitational, 1982; the Masters, 1986; and others.

He has been the recipient of awards including the PGA Player of the Year Award for 1967, 1972, 1973, 1975 and 1976; the Dunlop Professional Athlete of the Year Award for 1972; the Golfer of the Year (Professional Golfers' Association) Award for 1973; the Byron Nelson Award for 1964, 1965 and 1972; the Bob Jones Award for 1975; and *Sports Illustrated*'s Sportsman of the Year Award for 1978 and Athlete of the Decade Award for 1980. In addition to these and other honors, Jack Nicklaus was also named to the World Golf Hall of Fame.

Herbert Warren Wind feels that Jack Nicklaus has the ideal temperament for a golfer; during competition, he seems to actually enjoy the more intense situations, and is notably cooler and more relaxed than his peers. In Wind's words, his 'mind works unceasingly during a tournament round.' Despite his overwhelming commitment as a player and a course designer, Mr Nicklaus insists that he sees golf as a game, an enjoy-

able challenge, and not a life-and-death struggle.

He inherited his love of sports and much of his athletic ability from his father. Known to his friends as 'Charlie,' Jack's dad starred in high school football, basketball and baseball. He worked his way through college, and as a sophomore made some money as a linebacker for the Portsmouth (Ohio) Spartans, a pioneer National Football League team. He won the Columbus Public Courts tennis championship the year he graduated from college, and was a low-handicap golfer who modelled his swing on that of the legendary Bobby Jones.

Louis Charles Nicklaus was very close to his son Jack, and they played, watched and talked sports. This common thread remained unbroken through the time of the elder Nicklaus' death in 1970. To that time, Jack's father was always present to provide moral support at Jack's major events. Louis Nicklaus purposely removed his name tag from his tournament badge so that he could, without

At right: **The sixteenth green at Loxahatchee. Loxahatchee was chosen by** *Golf Digest* **as 'The Best New Private Course of the Year' for the year 1985.** *Below:* **Jack Nicklaus demonstrates his golfing expertise in playing out of a bunker.**

The recipient of an honorary Doctorate of Athletic Arts at Ohio State University in 1972, Jack Nicklaus has set down his thoughts about life and sports in the course of a writing career that began in 1964, and has produced a respectable number of books, including *My 55 Ways to Lower Your Golf Score*, *Take a Tip From Me*, *The Greatest Game of All*, *Golf My Way*, *The Best Way to Better Golf* (three volumes), *Jack Nicklaus' Lesson Tee*, *On and Off the Fairway*, *Jack Nicklaus' Playing Lessons* and *Playing Better Golf* (three volumes). In addition, his interest in the greater community led him to chair the Ohio Division of the American Cancer Society, and the Sports Division of the National Easter Seal Society, in 1967.

Jack Nicklaus would be the first to give credit where credit is due, and would not deny the considerable success that has been achieved in meaningful areas of his life. The careful nurturing of talent and ability, and the love of sports and all that matters in life are interdependently linked with the meticulous, challenging and fun course designs he has produced; they are products of that same sense of generosity, fairness, keen competition and careful thinking. Each layout possesses a fine, individual character of its own.

Mr Nicklaus has said, 'Building a golf course is my total expression. My golf game can only go on so long. But what I have learned can be put into a piece of ground to last beyond me.'

His first hole designs were actually redesigns that he did mentally as he played various courses—it was a way of finding an approach to take with each hole of each individual course, and it also helped him see where his own thinking differed from that of each individual course designer. He says that it helped him to be a better golfer, and, from our point of view, being a great golfer certainly gives him an advantage in the area of course design.

Jack began his formal design career as a consultant to golf course architects, and soon took up co-designing courses with such brilliant but seemingly contradictory architects as Pete Dye and Desmond Muirhead—with whom he collaborated in the building of several of the greatest courses in America, including Harbour Town Golf Links in South Carolina (with Dye), and the legendary Muirfield Village course in Ohio (with Muirhead). This diversity of collaboration gave him a strong and broad-based approach to golf course design. It was practical knowledge that he would come to use in his own business.

He decided to establish his own firm, and in 1973 he founded Jack Nicklaus Golf Services. Since then, Jack Nicklaus has established a global reputation for the brilliance and extremely fine execution of his designs.

the distraction of being recognized as a major player's father, watch his son play golf. Early on, he inculcated Jack with the phenomenal sense of fair play and true sportsmanship for which 'the Golden Bear' is known.

And, concerning his *own* role as a husband and father—Jack Nicklaus and Barbara Bash met at Ohio State in their freshman year, and were married in 1960. They have five children, who are, in declining order of seniority—Jack William II, Steven Charles, Nancy Jean, Gary Thomas and Michael Scott Nicklaus. Oldest son Jack Jr is a professional golfer, and son Gary is enjoying success on the collegiate golf team at his dad's alma mater.

Theirs is a very close and loving family. Jack Nicklaus has stated that his family comes first, even before golf, and he and Barbara are devoted parents, expecting their children to meet a certain wholesome standard of conduct, and encouraging their interests.

Barbara is tremendous support to him—a relaxed, intelligent woman who has a genius for organizing the very busy schedules at *chez* Nicklaus, and is herself extremely knowledgeable of sports (especially golf). For all intents and purposes, the Nicklauses are, have been, and seem likely to continue to be, marvelously stable in their family life, and very happily well-suited to one another. A secret of the 'golden touch' revealed—they have achieved what they have with care and patience, and with abiding single-mindedness.

Jack Nicklaus' early designs were cooperative efforts with other architects. *Above and left:* **Views of the Wabeek Country Club, a collaboration with Pete Dye.**

Among these are such renowned layouts and re-designs as The Australian Golf Club in Australia, St Mellion in Great Britain and the American courses Shoal Creek and Firestone South. With the exception of the still-new St Mellion course, all of the above (including the already-noted cooperative ventures with Dye and Muirhead) are included in *Golf* magazine's '100 Greatest Courses in the World.'

In addition, of the approximately 50 Nicklaus courses currently open for play, no less than 20 of them are featured in *Golf* magazine's listing of American golf courses, 'The Best Golf Courses in Each State,' with six Nicklaus courses—namely, Shoal Creek in Alabama; Desert Highlands in Arizona; Castle Pines in Colorado; Annandale in Mississippi; Muirfield Village in Ohio; and Park Meadows in Utah—given number one ranking in their respective states.

Jack Nicklaus feels that golf should be fun. While the uninformed assume that, given his powerful swing, Nicklaus probably designs courses that are huge and demand lots of strength, that is not the case. The Nicklaus design philosophy has three constants: golf should be much more a game of precision than of power; a course should reward a player who uses his mind ahead of his muscles; and a Nicklaus course design should disturb as little as possible what Mother Nature has made available to the designer.

This last dictum is a key to perceiving that Jack loves the Scottish tradition; his courses follow the lay of the land whenever possible, and often include such traditional features as double greens, Scottish-style bunkering and water hazards. Of course, they are built to embody the element of surprise.

Nicklaus courses are designed with such an eye to naturalness that ideal designs should appear 'as if they've been there forever.' In constructing a course within these parameters, original land contours, lakes, streams, trees and other interesting site features are incorporated into the design whenever possible. The course is therefore as complete as it could possibly be on the day that it opens; the maturation process then actually enhances the natural beauty of the design.

Notable examples of this 'lay of the land' design technique are Shoal Creek in Alabama, and Glen Abbey in Canada—with respective verdant settings that make both courses exquisitely beautiful, and very much a part of their surroundings. An example of a course that uses the same technique in a very different setting is the Desert Highlands Course in Arizona—where fairways follow the desert landscape, and saguaro cacti stand like sentinels above this beautiful newcomer in their midst.

A notable exception to this technique is the Nicklaus course at St Mellion Golf Club, in Cornwall, England—where the Nicklaus organization had to create the course hole-by-hole on an extremely steep hillside, and created an extremely beautiful, verdant and perilously challenging world-class golf course.

Beyond such artistic (and as in this last example, sometimes Herculean) construction efforts, Jack Nicklaus courses are designed for the people who will use them. As quoted in course material from the exquisite and exciting new Valhalla Golf Club in Kentucky, Jack Nicklaus says, 'I don't demand most courses to meet the needs of a big championship event such as the Memorial Tournament at Muirfield or the Canadian Open at Glen Abbey.'

He does believe in providing the player with an appropriate challenge. Nicklaus courses ask the golfer to think, and not only that, but each course is designed to be unique. A library of books on golf course design are but part of the resources that Jack Nicklaus uses in his endeavors to provide each layout with a good, balanced, mixture of shot values that are appropriate to the site, and to the players who will actually be using the course. Varying tee placements add flexibility to the designs, allowing players of a wide range of abilities to find their level of challenge on each course.

Mr Nicklaus declares, in a publicity release from the Park Meadows Country Club, 'A good golf course is one that serves its intended purpose. If it's built for private use, as with condominium owners, then it must serve that function... .' In the same interview, he goes on to say of his courses that 'They're all geared toward the amateur player, who's going to play them on a year-round basis. If you're going to have a tournament, you build in the capacity to house a tournament... .'

At the beginning stages of design, Jack Nicklaus sets down the basic landforms, shapes and routings that will go into the course, and these will not change during course construction. However, during the building of the course—which can sometimes take three years due to permit complications and other important details—his concepts may change. Beyond the established basics, his periodic tours of the construction site may

well result in changes of secondary elements, such as foliage and bunkers.

The Nicklaus method of ensuring design freshness and the uniqueness of each course is quite interesting. If one of his design associates or assistants can second-guess him as to what a course feature will be, he changes that feature, to promote the element of surprise, and to prevent stereotypical thinking from creeping into his creative processes.

Above all else, he wants to 'create good golf courses.' And create them he does—around the world. So far, Jack Nicklaus and his associates have completed 51 courses throughout the continental US and Hawaii, and also in Canada, the British West Indies, Japan, Spain and England; an additional 17 courses are under construction in the US, Switzerland, Austria and Japan; and 20 courses are currently under contract in the US, Japan, Indonesia, Italy and France.

The Jack Nicklaus organization includes one group that handles Jack's business affairs, another that deals with course design, another that handles course construction, and another that is responsible for management and maintenance of the finished product—to ensure that, not only will a championship-quality golf course retain its quality, but it will not be a burden to club members who, after all, want to spend their leisure time playing golf, not attending maintenance committee meetings.

Course owners are able to engage Jack Nicklaus Clubmanagement to provide lasting service for all fairways, greens and other aspects of the course, as well as taking care of the club's organizational details overall,

including the actual management of the golf club itself.

Jack Nicklaus' stated goal as a golf course architect is 'to make the people I work for successful.' When queried by the editors of the *Park City Lodestar* as to whether he would rather leave a legacy as a great *golfer*, or as a great *golf course designer*, he answered, 'Both of them sound fine to me. Anything I try, I do to the best of my ability... so far, people have been very good about giving me the ability to control what I put on a piece of ground on a golf course.'

Jack Nicklaus is extremely good at whatever he does. As a brilliant course architect, he is part of an elite group, just as being at the very pinnacle of his profession as a golfer places him in yet another elite group, as does being a devoted parent. The most astonishing thing is that everywhere you look in literature that is about Jack Nicklaus, you find nary a discouraging word. He's so well-rounded, and so modest about it, that you could run into him on the street without knowing who he is and think, 'Gee, what a nice guy.'

So, here's to Jack Nicklaus, golf course designer and golfer *par excellence*—a man who makes the old saying, 'Win or lose, what matters is how you go about it,' ring true as gold. And, just as playing his magnificent courses has brought a treasure trove of top-notch golfing to golfers of all levels, excellence is the very hallmark of the man they call 'the Golden Bear.'

Below: **The fourteenth green of The Bear at Grand Traverse Village.** *At right:* **The twelfth of Cochise, one of three Nicklaus courses at Desert Mountain.**

The World of Jack Nicklaus

The golf courses listed below have been (a) designed, (b) co-designed, (c) redesigned by Jack Nicklaus, or (d) redesigned by Jack Nicklaus Golf Services. Those listed in **boldface** are those which were in play by 1988. Others are under contract and/or under development. The year listed is the one in which the course was opened.

GLEN ABBEY GOLF CLUB (1976) (a)
Toronto, Canada

BRITANNIA GOLF CLUB (1985) (a)
Cayman Islands, BWI

KIELE CLASSIC GOLF CLUB (a)
Kauai, Hawaii
WESTIN KAUAI GOLF COURSE (a)
Kauai, Hawaii

SAINT MELLION (1986) (a)
Plymouth, England
GOLF DE VILLEPREUX (a)
Paris, France
GOLF CLUB CRANS (a)
Crans-sur-Sierre, Switzerland
GOLF CLUB GUT ALTENTANN (a)
Salzburg, Austria
LA MORALEJA GOLF CLUB (1976) (b)
(with Desmond Muirhead)
Madrid, Spain

COSTA SMERALDA (a)
Sardinia, Italy

NEW SAINT ANDREWS (1973) (b)
(with Desmond Muirhead)
Ohtawara City, Japan
KAZUSA GOLF CLUB (1984) (a)
Kimitsu City, Japan
IWAMA GOLF COURSE (a)
Iwama, Japan
JAPAN MEMORIAL GOLF CLUB (a)
Kobe City, Japan
SAINT CREEK (a)
Nagoya, Japan
SHIMONOSEKI GOLDEN GOLF CLUB (a)
Yamaguchi, Japan
SUNNYFIELD (a)
Tokyo, Japan

BUMI SERPONG DAMAI (a)
Jakarta, Indonesia

AUSTRALIAN GOLF CLUB (1977) (c)
Sydney, Australia

The golf courses listed below have been (a) designed, (b) co-designed, (c) redesigned by Jack Nicklaus, or (d) redesigned by Jack Nicklaus Golf Services. Those listed in **boldface** are those which were in play by 1988. Others are under contract and/or under development. The year listed is the one in which the course was opened.

PARK MEADOWS (1983) (a)
Park City, Utah

BRECKENRIDGE GOLF CLUB (1987) (a)
Breckenridge, Colorado
CASTLE PINES (RESIDENTS COURSE) (1987) (a)
Castle Rock, Colorado
CASTLE PINES GOLF CLUB (1981) (a)
Denver, Colorado
MERIDIAN GOLF CLUB (1984) (a)
Denver, Colorado
COUNTRY CLUB OF THE ROCKIES (1984) (a)
Vail, Colorado
PTARMIGAN GOLF CLUB (a)
Fort Collins, Colorado

BEAR CREEK GOLF CLUB (1982) (a)
Wildomar, California
CAPE MALIBU RESORT(a)
Oxnard, California
COUNTRY CLUB AT MORNINGSIDE (1982) (a)
Palm Sorings, California
DOVE CANYON (a)
Mission Viejo, California
GOLF CLUB AT MALIBU (a)
Malibu, California
PGA WEST (MEMBERS COURSE) (1987) (a)
La Quinta, California
PGA WEST (RESORT COURSE) (1987) (a)
La Quinta, California

DESERT HIGHLANDS (1984) (a)
Pinnacle Peak, Arizona
DESERT MOUNTAIN (COCHISE) (1987) (a)
Scottsdale, Arizona
DESERT MOUNTAIN (RENEGADE) (1987) (a)
Scottsdale, Arizona
DESERT MOUNTAIN (GERONIMO) (a)
Scottsdale, Arizona
LA PALOMA (1984) (a)
Tuscon, Arizona

GRAND TRAVERSE RESORT (1984) (a)
Traverse City, Michigan
GRAND TRAVERSE RESORT (a)
(Additional 18 holes)
Grand Traverse, Michigan
WABEEK GOLF CLUB (1972) (b)
(with Pete Dye)
Bloomfield Hills, Michigan

SAINT ANDREWS GOLF CLUB (1985) (c)
Hastings-on-Hudson, New York

SYCAMORE HILLS GOLF COURSE
Fort Wayne, Indiana

COUNTRY CLUB AT MUIRFIELD (1982) (a)
Dublin, Ohio
JACK NICKLAUS SPORTS CENTER (1973) (b)
(with Desmond Muirhead)
Cincinnati, Ohio
MUIRFIELD VILLAGE GOLF CLUB (1974) (a)
(with Desmond Muirhead)

WYNSTONE COUNTRY CLUB (a)
North Barrington, Illinois

AMERICANA LAKE GENEVA RESORT (1970) (b)
(with Pete Dye)
Lake Geneva, Wisconsin

GREENBRIER COURSE (1978) (c)
White Sulphur Springs, West Virginia

GOVERNORS CLUB (a)
Chapel Hill, North Carolina
PINEHURST NATIONAL (a)
Pinehurst, North Carolina
ELK RIVER (1984) (a)
Banner Elk, North Carolina
LONG BAY CLUB (a)
North Myrtle Beach, South Carolina
PAWLEYS PLANTATION (a)
Pawleys Island, South Carolina
MELROSE (1987) (a)
Daufuskie Island, South Carolina
TURTLE POINT (1981) (a)
Kiawah Island, South Caroiina
HARBOUR TOWN LINKS (1970) (b)
(with Pete Dye)
Hilton Head, South Carolina

VALHALLA (1986) (a)
Louisville, Kentucky

RICHLAND COUNTRY CLUB (a)
Nashville, Tennessee

SHOAL CREEK (1976) (a)
Birmingham, Alabama

COUNTRY CLUB OF THE SOUTH (1987) (a)
Atlanta, Georgia

DALLAS ATHLETIC CLUB (1986) (c)
Dallas, Texas
DALLAS ATHLETIC CLUB (GOLD COURSE) (a)
Dallas, Texas
HILLS OF LAKEWAY (1981) (a)
Austin, Texas
LOCHINVAR GOLF CLUB (1980) (a)
Houston, Texas

ANNANDALE GOLF CLUB (1981) (a)
Baton Rouge, Louisiana

ENGLISH TURN (a)
New Orleans, Louisiana

GRAND CYPRESS RESORT (LINKS COURSE) (1987) (a)
Orlando, Florida
GRAND CYPRESS RESORT (1984) (a)
Orlando, Florida
BEAR'S PAW GOLF CLUB (1980) (a)
Naples, Florida
JOHN'S ISLAND (1970) (b)
(with Pete Dye)
Vero Beach, Florida
SAILFISH POINT (1981) (a)
Hutchinson Island, Florida
LOXAHATCHEE (1984) (a)
Jupiter, Florida
MAYACOO LAKES GOLF CLUB (1973) (b)
(with Desmond Muirhead)
West Palm Beach, Florida
BEAR LAKES (1985) (a)
West Palm Beach, Florida
BEAR LAKES (LINKS COURSE) (a)
West Palm Beach, Florida

The Briar Patch at Americana Lake Geneva Resort

Lake Geneva, Wisconsin USA

Before Jack Nicklaus had gone into golf course designing on his own, Jack Nicklaus collaborated on a number of courses with Pete Dye. The 6742-yard Briar Patch Golf Course at the Americana Lake Geneva Resort is one of the results of this very fruitful cooperation. The course opened in 1971, and has recently been judged as one of 'The Top Five Courses in the Midwest' by *Golf Digest*.

Described by some as 'the undiscovered pleasure of the Midwest,' the Briar Patch is a Scottish-influenced course featuring a double green (shared by holes eight and twelve), rolling hills and river beds throughout. A breath of fresh air in Wisconsin, the Americana Lake Geneva Resort has something for everyone: a complete Fitness Centre plus sports, dining and entertainment. It is also the home of the famed 7200 yard par 72 'Brute' Golf Course, designed by Robert Bruce Harris.

Varying tee settings give this course a tremendous variety of play. The following is a hole-by-hole description of The Briar Patch.

Hole number one plays as a dogleg right from the back tees, but is straightaway from the forward tees. Large earth bunkers guard either side of the green and the green approach. The wide but shallow green will be hard to hold on to.

The second hole features a carry over a large earth bunker that contains numerous small sand bunkers to a landing area that has a distracting pond off to the right. The green approach involves a sizable earth bunker in front and on the right front of the green, and a small earth bunker at the left rear will increase the chances that you'll be chipping out of a bunker on this one. Hole number three is a dogleg right with a bunker wedged into the front of the broad, shallow green.

The fourth hole, a par three, is one of Wisconsin's most challenging golf holes. A river

Below: **A golfer tees off at hole number three. The Briar Patch has recently been ranked in the top five of the Midwest.** *Above right:* **'Playing through' at the Briar Patch. Compare this photo with the course map.**

winds down along the left side of the tee, and then cuts across in front of the green. With water at right, left and in front of the green, and bunkers in back and at left, the green is surrounded by hazards.

Hole number five is a dogleg left, with a large earth-and-sand bunker on its left, and an obliquely-situated green that is sandwiched between two treacherous bunkers. The sixth hole is a near-90 degree dogleg left with bunkering left and right on the green approach and strategically situated at right and at left rear of a small, shallow green.

The seventh hole is a par three with a challenging green. Hole number eight shares a double green with hole number twelve. With two tee positions and an expansive, irregularly-shaped green protected by bunkers at rear and at right, hole number eight will test your accuracy.

The ninth hole is a dogleg left with water on either side of the fairway. The distractions and hazards presented here demand special concentration. Hole number ten plays straightaway to an obliquely-set green. The eleventh is a double dogleg—right, then left—with an earth-and-sand bunker on the right that squeezes the landing area down to a very tight spot indeed, with a massive earth-and-sand bunker on the green approach necessitating a carry to a small and slippery green.

Hole number twelve is a par three that shares an expansive double green with hole eight. This hole will test your putting skills. The thirteenth hole is complete with variant tee settings. It's a dogleg left with a broad bunker across the face of a wide but shallow green. Hole number fourteen has variant tee settings, and plays as a dogleg left from the back tee, and as a straightaway hole from the forward tee. A small green, a bunker on the right of the green approach and a bunker on the left of the green create a test of accuracy here.

The fifteenth hole presents golfers with a lake carry off the tees. A small, pear-shaped green presents itself 'stem first' on this exciting and challenging dogleg left. Hole number sixteen, with variant tee settings, can be played either as a dogleg right from the for-

ward tees, or as a straightaway hole from the back tees. Golfers at the back tees must make a carry over the edge of a lake on the left. The green is deep and extremely narrow; on both sides are longitudinal bunkers. Accuracy is the key here.

Hole number seventeen is a par three with variant tee settings, all of which feature a lake carry to a broad, shallow green. Golfers at the tees of the eighteenth hole must shoot over a river to a landing area that is just right of a huge earth-and-sand bunker, the tip of which must be carried over to an irregularly-shaped green having a bunker all along its rear portion. It's a great hole with which to finish a challenging and rewarding round of golf.

Hole	1	2	3	4	5	6	7	8	9	Out	
Blue	388	519	452	210	369	544	123	369	463	3437	
White	342	472	419	170	355	524	114	351	456	3203	
Red	319	456	380	81	304	423	93	333	326	2715	
Par	4	5	4	3	4	5	3	4	4	36	
Hole	10	11	12	13	14	15	16	17	18	In	Total
Blue	335	607	201	423	408	363	385	148	435	3305	6742
White	326	580	173	408	372	327	369	134	425	3114	6317
Red	256	555	120	363	331	280	349	116	323	2693	5408
Par	4	5	3	4	4	4	4	3	4	35	71

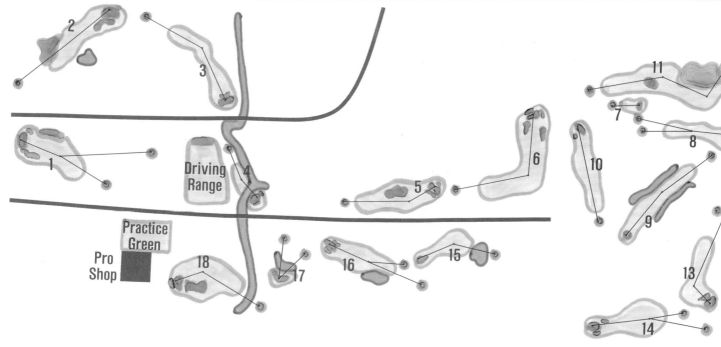

The Australian Golf Club

Kensington, Australia

J ack Nicklaus was invited to submit ideas for the enhancement of this course in 1976. The construction work began in 1977 under Mr Nicklaus' personal supervision, and resulted in a recontouring and reconfiguring of the course. The Australian was chosen to be among *Golf* magazine's '100 Greatest Courses in the World' in September of 1987.

The introduction of numerous water carries and the replanting of the fairways with the new hybrid Couch 329 changed the course from what had been a wind-swept, virtually treeless linksland course to a lushly tree-lined layout similar to many American courses. The changes essentially have added challenge to this venerable course.

Jack worked in cooperation with Mr Kerry Packer, the sponsor of the Australian Open–which is now permanently based at the Australian Golf Club course. A bit of historical review on this layout may give an inkling as to the kind of excitement that the remodeling project generated. The Australian Golf Club–one of the most prestigious clubs in Austra-lia–was founded in 1882, at which time golfers played on a course situated near the present-day Sydney Cricket Ground. This location was not quite what was needed, so a further venue for play was sought.

After a search for a suitable site, 99 acres of land were leased on the shore of Botany Bay, an inlet of the Tasman Sea, just southwest of Sydney. Here, two distinguished firsts were inaugurated–the Country Golf Week Tournament, and the Australian Open Championship. In 1903, the club bought the present

site–175 acres in Kensington, which is due south of Sydney. The original eighteen hole design at Kensington was the result of a competition between three professional golfers who are known to us as 'Hutchinson, Martin and Carnegie Clark.' Alterations to this design were made in 1926 at the suggestion of renowned course designer Dr A MacKenzie.

Tragedy struck in 1932, when the clubhouse–then located at the present sixth tee area–was completely destroyed by fire. The new clubhouse was built on newly purchased land to the west of the then-existing layout, and this necessitated further changes to accommodate the first and tenth tees in the vicinity of the new building. In 1967 the club was informed that a freeway, known as Southern Cross Drive, was to be built on the course's western and southern boundaries. This freeway would connect Kingsford-Smith Airport with Sydney. The necessary course changes were designed by Sloan Morpeth. Then came the hand of Jack Nicklaus, and the transformation wrought thereby has added challenge to this, which was already one of Australia's finest courses.

After a second total fire loss of their clubhouse–before the Nicklaus course changes were completed–a more modern clubhouse was built on the original clubhouse site.

This beautiful course is adorned with flowers at aesthetically advantageous points, and has hosted a plethora of national and state championships, both amateur and professional, in addition to many commercial tournaments. This great course will no doubt only grow in stature as the years continue to roll by. The following is a hole-by-hole description of this fine golf course, which measures 6443 meters from the back tees.

Hole number one is a tree-lined dogleg right having four bunkers situated on its inside 'knee.' The fairway then veers back to the left for a pinched green approach, and a well-bunkered green. The second hole is a well-wooded par three featuring longitudinal bunkers to the right and left of the two-tiered green. Hole three is the first of the water holes. This par four doglegs left at a cluster of bunkers–two right, one left–and bends around the edge of a lake to the right. A dogleg right brings you to the split-level green, which has bunkers at left and behind, and the lake to the right.

The par three fourth hole plays around the same lake that we met on the previous hole. You tee off to a fairway which bends right around the limb of the lake, which provides most golfers with an obvious water carry for a savings on strokes to the green, which itself is bunkered left and right. Hole number five, at 526 meters, is the longest hole on the course. A tree-lined par five, its opposing bunkers at the first dogleg introduce a long fairway that will give you a good chance to test your driving abilities. A trickily bunkered, two-level

Below: **The daunting, beautiful vista on the approach to The Australian's tough seventeenth green.**

green provides a satisfying target to conclude this hole.

Hole six gives you a 'gunsight' of trees to aim at the fairway with–straight and narrow here. The fairway features a ridge early on, and has a massive bunker to the right front of the split-level green. You tee off down a hall-way of trees on the seventh hole, and unless your shot tends to the right or lays up, you'll find the two fairway bunkers lying left. The split-level green is situated snugly beside a lake. The tees of hole eight are sandwiched between two lakes, and staggered, opposing bunkers guard the fairway early on. This hole's asymmetrical, two-level green is bunk-ered left and right of its narrow 'jaw.'

The ninth hole fairway bends to the left, with a bunker set to the left of its 'knee.' Bunkers right and left of the green keep shots straight and narrow; a long lake to the left beyond the bunkering should keep your calcu-lations toward not letting shots go too far afield. Trees and an access road are to your right. Well treed, par four hole ten leads you past two right-lying fairway bunkers to a green having a slope at right and behind, and a cannily-placed bunker at left. Hole eleven, a par three, has trees all along its left, and a 32 meters-long green. This green is very well bunkered.

The twelfth hole has you teeing off into a dogleg surrounded with bunkers. Down the tree-lined fairway from this is a two-level green with bunkering right and left. The golfer tees off down a long hallway of trees on hole thirteen. These trees compose a daunting psychological barrier, as they tend to force tee shots to the rough and trees at left, not to mention the large fairway bunker that lies just beyond the fairway's dogleg. The green is elevated, with bunkers set right and left in the approach.

Hole fourteen, a reasonable par five at 512 meters, forms a long serpentine. You tee off somewhat obliquely to a fairway which has two bunkers on its right to catch overlong tee shots. A long bunker guards the right of the green approach, and the green itself is bunk-ered at front–left and right. The green is also backed directly into several trees, and *that* could mean trouble! The fifteenth hole, a par three, features a split-level green that is vir-tually surrounded by three hefty bunkers. The sixteenth is tree-lined all the way, and has a gang of bunkers on the right front of the green, and two more on the left rear. This three-tiered green is obliquely set and oblong– be careful here.

Hole number seventeen winds you up for the conclusion. Shots from the back tee are forced to the left of a fairway which fades to

At right: **The Australian's fourth hole, a challenging par three. This is a view of the green, from the far side of a lake that figures in play.**

the right–not much to land on from that perspective! Trees on both sides line this hole, and the fairway bends left to tuck the green partially behind a left-lying lake. Bunkers on either side of the green complete the scenario for a spine-tingling challenge. The tree-lined eighteenth bends to the right, for a balancing act with the previous hole. A fairway bunker squeezes in from the right early on, and hummocks on the left give a hint of Scottish linksland. Nearing the green, two left-lying bunkers guard the outside of the fairway bend, and a longitudinal lake guards the inside of same. The green has a bunker on its left, and widens away from the lake (which guards the green from the right), toward the trees behind it. It's a cleverly arranged set of defenses, and is sure to provide an exhilarating and challenging finish for your round of golf at The Australian Golf Club.

Above: The skyline of Sydney is a backdrop for northeastern vistas at The Australian. *At right:* This monumental composition features the bunkers that guard the sixteenth green approach. Your view of the green could be similar if your attention lapses. Even so, the beauty of the course is evident.

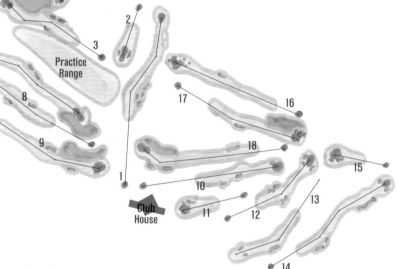

Note: all distances given in meters

Hole	1	2	3	4	5	6	7	8	9	Out	
Member Blue	457	168	343	159	526	384	382	397	405	3221	
Member White	440	156	327	136	497	378	320	387	388	3029	
Associate 403		146	291	105	453	366	312	379	305	2760	
Par	5	3	4	3	5	4/5	4	4/5	4	36/38	

Hole	10	11	12	13	14	15	16	17	18	In	Total
Member Blue	379	173	367	351	512	187	388	390	475	3222	6443
Member White	361	140	354	346	490	173	368	359	459	3050	6079
Associate	313	120	278	325	465	152	353	309	430	2745	5505
Par	4	3	4	4	5	3	4/5	4	5	36/37	72/75

Below: The Australian Golf Club seventeenth green, with a perspective down the fairway. The playability, challenge and aesthetic qualities of this course are of the highest level. *Golf* magazine ranked this course among 'The 100 Greatest Courses in the World.'

Breckenridge Golf Club

Breckenridge, Colorado USA

Spectacularly situated in the midst of the Rocky Mountains, this scenic course offers golfers more than a lion's share of exquisite mountain vistas, including the Ten Mile Range to the west; the Gore Range to the northwest; the Williams Fork Range to the north; and the Front Range to the east.

In addition to the mountain scenery, various forms of wildlife live on or frequent the course. Deer, elk, fox, red-tail hawks and beaver are among the resident fauna here. Flowers are evident in profusion, with the Colorado State Flower, the Columbine, most visible by the 15th tee boxes.

The golf course is almost 7300 yards from the championship tees. The elevation here, though, is 9300-plus feet, and this high alti-

Above: **The Breckenridge welcome sign.** *Below:* **Going for the pin at the eighteenth green.** *At right:* **A dramatic, Rocky Mountain vista at Breckenridge.**

tude will give ball flights as much as a 15 percent extra boost. Some 48 bunkers add to the challenge at Breckenridge Golf Club, and the streams and lakes which come into play on 12 holes are fed from snow melt and natural springs.

Construction began on the golf course in 1982. The land in its natural state was deemed a natural wetlands by the US Army Corps of Engineers. Because of the ecological value of such wetlands areas, the Town of Breckenridge and the Corps of Engineers worked together to develop new wetlands areas along the Blue River north of town.

The course is owned and operated by the Town of Breckenridge, and therefore has the distinction of being the only municipally

Below: **The greens are impeccable, and the surroundings are spectacular at Breckenridge.** *At right:* **A challenging and scenic green. This golfing facility has mountain vistas everywhere you look.**

owned Nicklaus-designed course in the world today. The front nine opened for play on 1 June 1985; the course was closed in September of 1985 because of a water drainage problem with the putting greens, and was reopened with all 18 holes in play on 1 June 1987. This is, as is mentioned above, a wetlands course, and you will have plenty of natural distractions and defenses to meet: this Nicklaus design, like Nicklaus designs the world over, incorporates the native environment into the beauty and defense scheme of the course. Following is a brief hole-by-hole description of this exciting new golf course.

All but the innermost tee of hole number one have a stream carry, with the back positions carrying over two streams! The fairway bends to the right around two large bunkers. The green has two bunkers to its right, and one bunker on its left. Hole two has a snake's-head shaped green at the end of a long, undulating fairway. Guarding the green are three bunkers at left and one right.

Hole three is a 403-yard dogleg right. The lake following the fairway's curving inner surface guarantees a water carry for all but the most cautious of players. Bunkers at right front and at rear guard the green here. Par

three hole four plays to a narrow fairway and a kidney bean-shaped green. A bunker to the rear of the green is positioned so as to catch overflights. The fifth bulges to the left and then narrows toward the green–it could be a tricky hole to calculate. The green is set obliquely, and has a bunker at right rear.

Hole number six is a study in varied approaches to play. The main fairway describes a shallow double dogleg with a long bunker early on, on its right. Near the green approach, a smaller auxiliary fairway appears at the left. You can play down the large fairway all the way, or play to the auxiliary, thus creating an entirely different green approach. The green, which starts out narrow and widens toward the rear, is set obliquely to the primary fairway, and is head-on to the auxiliary. Two bunkers on the green's left complete the scenario.

Hole seven, a par three, features a stream carry–between the halves of a split fairway. The green is set trickily at the nethermost lobe of the second half–a challenging target. Hole eight plays along a stream, which rides along the fairway's right, and then, at the green approach, cuts across to the left. Tee shots are challenged by the stream at right and a large, strategically placed bunker at left. The small green lies on the other side of the stream, and its two rear-lying bunkers further call you to do your best.

Tee shots are again challenged with a bunker at hole nine. The fairway tapers away to the right toward the well-bunkered green. Take a break here–for the tees at hole ten must carry a considerable length of serpentine stream that seems to magnetize your ball to the freshwater depths. Hole eleven is a dogleg right to an irregularly shaped green having a bunker at its right. The twelfth forms a dogleg left, with a bunker on its right–just where many tee shots will find it. At 580 yards from the back tees, this is the longest hole at Breckenridge. The fairway plays along a stream up to the green approach, which features a carry over same. On the 'other side' is a small, ovoid green with a bunker at right rear.

The thirteenth hole, a par three, features highly varied tee locations, with a small bunker just off the tip of the fairway. The fairway itself seems calculated to cause optical illusion, as it fades to the right. The green is set obliquely, end-on, and has water to its left and

Above: **At Breckenridge, it sometimes seems that you're playing golf in the midst of the sky.** *These pages:* **Views of Breckenridge Golf Club: a challenge,** *and* **your shots will travel farther at this altitude.**

bunkers at right and at rear. Hole fourteen is an unusually configured hole, with a massive bunker preceding the fairway, at right. The fairway begins as a mere stem at the rear of this bunker, and proceeds to the left, then makes a right angle to form a fairway proper. All tee shots here have a stream carry, with the back tee carrying over *two* streams. The fairway, in addition to having the aforementioned premonitive bunker, has another right-lying bunker halfway down. The oval green is protected by bunkers at left and right.

Long hole fifteen plays down a fairway having bunkers strategically set along its left perimeter. The sixteenth hole's green is surrounded on three sides by a horseshoe bunker, and additionally has a small bunker at rear. There's lots of sand on this par three. The seventeenth hole's tees face a triumvirate of bunkers on the fairway approach—and the offset green, with an opposing bunker to the left, should set you nicely for very exciting hole number eighteen.

Tee shots on hole eighteen face the first half of a split fairway. A large bunker lying right could pull the wayward shot in, especially since a left-lying lake dictates that 'right' is the way to go here. Some golfers may want to carry over the stream and try for the green at this point, but bunkers at front, rear and right of the green–and the lake immediately to its left–make for a very challenging strategic situation, and you'll probably want to lay up here. Any way you play it, it's a memorable conclusion to a fine eighteen holes of golf.

Below: **A view down the ninth fairway toward the green and the Breckenridge clubhouse.** *At right:* **This view from the seventh green to the clubhouse points up the skillfully melded, natural flavor of the course.**

Hole	1	2	3	4	5	6	7	8	9	Out	
Nicklaus	403	554	403	214	416	549	224	461	473	3697	
Tournament	335	509	384	175	373	504	186	399	461	3346	
Regular	337	496	345	158	329	460	168	344	418	3055	
Ladies'	251	442	289	120	273	435	142	307	344	2603	
Par	4	5	4	3	4	5	3	4	4	36	
Hole	**10**	**11**	**12**	**13**	**14**	**15**	**16**	**17**	**18**	**In**	**Total**
Nicklaus	405	409	580	200	410	562	177	416	423	3582	7279
Tournament	310	398	503	200	396	533	160	385	345	3230	6576
Regular	280	346	482	172	384	489	112	345	315	2925	5980
Ladies'	233	317	408	124	304	459	75	264	279	2463	5066
Par	4	4	5	3	4	5	3	4	4	36	72

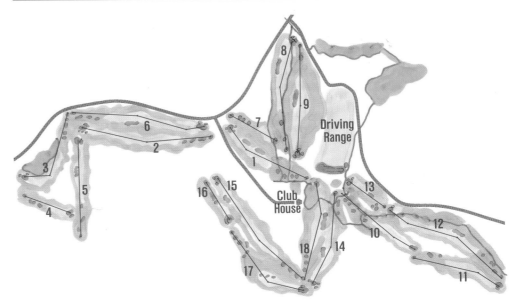

These pages: **Scenic surroundings and excellent course design make the Breckenridge Golf Club a great golf experience—in the Colorado Rocky Mountains.**

Castle Pines Golf Club

Castle Rock, Colorado USA

Chosen as one of the best 130 courses in the USA by the American Society of Golf Course Architects for several years running, Castle Pines Golf Club is the more demanding of two fine golf courses designed by Jack Nicklaus for the Castle Pines Land Company—the other being the Country Club of Castle Pines, which is the subject of the course discussion that immediately follows this one.

Back in the early 1970s, sports aficionado and businessman *par excellence* Jack A Vickers envisioned a classic golf complex to be located within the scrub oak and pine forest just north of Castle Rock.

Though it took years to acquire the 5000 acre parcel upon which to build his dream, Mr Vickers' determination and acumen carried the day. He wanted a layout that would take an honored place at the forefront of international golfing. He wisely chose as his layout designer golfing legend and renowned course architect Jack Nicklaus. Together the two of them carefully surveyed the entire site.

Their main objective was a course that would challenge the professional and still be a fair and enjoyable test of golfing skills for club members. Construction began in 1979, seeding was accomplished in 1981, and the course was opened for play in October of that same

year. Mr Vickers then brought together 12 distinguished men–including his world-famous architect, Jack Nicklaus–to serve as 'Founders' of Castle Pines, and they established a membership policy similar to that of the Augusta National Golf Club in Georgia.

The stature of Castle Pines in world golfing circles is yet to be determined, but it is already rated as the most challenging in Colorado, as well as the most scenic. Castle Pines hosts 'The International,' a yearly tournament featuring 162 of the finest professional golfers in

Below: **A view of hole number five—the toughest hole on a course that is rated the most challenging in Colorado.** *At right:* **The eighteenth and the clubhouse.**

Above: **An aerial view of the eighth at Castle Pines Golf Club.** *At right:* **The green and the approach at the fifteenth hole. Bunkers lie beyond the green.**

the world. The International's scoring system is such that greater than normal rewards are given for birdies and eagles—which encourages aggressive play, to the excitement of players and audience alike. The field is reduced daily through the first four days of play, leaving 18 finalists to compete for a purse which is the single richest day in golfing–the prize for 1988 was $750,000. Competing golfers play for daily prizes in addition to the final purse.

This course is a monument to the designing talents of Jack Nicklaus. Its jewel-like presence was carved out of very difficult, rocky terrain, and it flows around and through stands of native scrub oak and Ponderosa pine. Castle Pines, renowned for its beauty and high level of play, was built without making major alterations to the appearance and ecological balance of its locale; rather like a Henry Moore sculpture, the eye of the artist saw the inherent shape in the unpolished form.

At 7503 yards and par 72, this is an awesome course. Yet its 6600 foot altitude not only provides fresh, invigorating mountain air, but the very thinness of that mountain air allows hit balls to travel 10 percent further than they would at lower altitudes. Built for championship play, and built to be enjoyed by the average golfer as well, the layout at Castle Pines Golf Club seems destined for the realm of golfing legend. The following is a hole-by-hole description of this excellent golf course.

Hole number one is a 644-yard par five that could grant you an eagle if you play your second shot right. If that shot goes awry, however, the three bunkers on the left of the

These pages: **A view of the Castle Pines Golf Club seventh hole. The vistas here seem to roll on for miles, and the rustic outbuildings add a historical touch.**

green approach could become an unwelcome haven. Hole two is striking visually because of the long, serpentine trap, in the form of a culvert or dry wash, which winds up alongside it and cuts over in front of the green. The green here is narrow and difficult and, in addition to the trap, is bunkered right and left and has hazard behind.

Number three, a par four, feels like the wide open spaces, and has a brush-filled culvert and two bunkers to deal with at the green. You tee off to a fairway which is split by a mean-

dering trap similar to that we encountered at hole two. In addition, the back tee has a tree directly in the line of sight for what would be a good carry over the trap to the second half of fairway.

The fourth is a par three that plays across the aforementioned trap to an oval green having a largish bunker behind it, in line with your shot. You'll need to stop on a dime.

Keith Schneider, the head professional at Castle Pines, is quoted in the course brochure as saying that the fifth hole is the toughest on

the course. It plays uphill and is 477 yards at par four. 'The length, the collection bunker and the green make it tough,' says Schneider. The collection bunker is one of a plethora of bunkers on the green approach here. In addition, there is an auxiliary fairway paralleling the main fairway at the green approach–as was noted on hole fourteen in the Breckenridge Golf Club portion of this book.

Above: **The idyllic-looking eleventh green.** *Below:* **A golfer plays out of a bunker during a tournament.** *At right:* **The sixteenth's elevated green.**

When you tee off at hole six, your ball will find a fairway which has a 'gunsight' composed of opposing sets of bunkers. Another bunker is set directly in the green approach. Hole seven is a par three whose green has two large bunkers out front and two smaller bunkers behind. Despite the long distance from the tees to the fairway, the eighth is a possible birdie, with a graceful, right-arcing fairway.

The following quote from Keith Schneider in the club brochure is an apt description of hole number nine: '… a tough driving hole with water on the right, trouble left, then a blind uphill second shot to a mean green–a tough target.' The tenth plays 485 yards downhill from the back tees. A very threatening pond means a carry on the green approach, and bunkers at left and right rear of the green complete the difficulties awaiting players here. It's an invigorating, challenging hole.

The par three eleventh hole features a carry over a drainage ditch to a green having one large crescent bunker on its right front. Hole number twelve plays to a fairway on which you will want to carefully calculate your shot to the green–which has two bunkers set to catch approach shots, and a rushing stream and trees to provide additional hazard. Hole thirteen describes a shallow dogleg right to a well-bunkered and not easy to hit green.

Hole fourteen, at 595 yards the second longest hole on the course, features a shallow dogleg left, and at the end of the longer of its two fairway segments, a drainage ditch carry. From the second fairway segment, it's a straighforward shot to a green which is bunkered at left front and at rear. Hole fifteen is a dogleg right in earnest, ending with a green that is sandwiched between a lake on the right and three bunkers on the left.

The sixteenth is a par three that demands your all. Again, from Keith Schneider, in course brochure: 'If they miss this green, it's very difficult to get up and down for your par. The collection bunker front left and an elevated green make chipping next to impossible.' Hole seventeen drives away from a lake– in fact, the back tee has water on three sides– down a long, left-arcing fairway, to a green which hides behind a row of bunkers.

The eighteenth hole is a grand driving hole, a 480-yard par four, which curves gently to the left. A squad of 10 bunkers keeps you from being too daring in shaving strokes off your score, and the three bunkers–at left front, right front and rear–protecting the green will ensure that this will be a challenge *indeed* with which to complete your round of golf at Castle Pines.

Hole	1	2	3	4	5	6	7	8	9	Out	
Championship	644	408	452	205	477	417	185	535	458	3781	
Regular	600	379	413	171	393	380	145	507	431	3419	
Middle	506	329	352	149	349	358	121	479	350	2993	
Forward	454	276	307	117	330	341	100	445	333	2703	
Par	5	4	4	3	4	4	3	5	4	36	
Hole	10	11	12	13	14	15	16	17	18	In	Total
Championship	485	197	422	439	595	403	209	492	480	3722	7503
Regular	460	186	382	394	550	355	188	470	430	3415	6834
Middle	400	171	331	346	367	302	165	436	361	2979	5972
Forward	370	140	325	313	449	274	140	351	317	2679	5382
Par	4	3	4	4	5	4	3	5	4	36	72

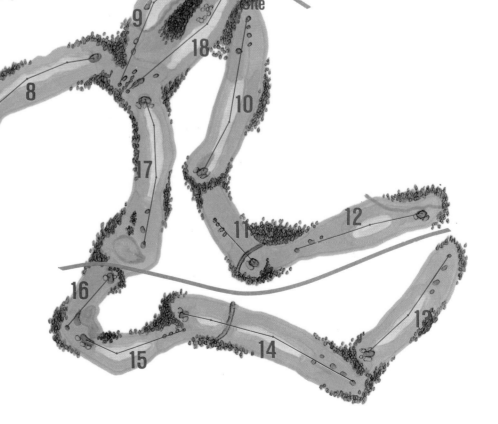

Above left: **Looking back toward the fairway from the green of the twelfth hole; note the stream to one side of the green. At the high altitude of this course, hit balls travel 10 percent farther than at lower elevations.** *At left:* **When the sun is low, a golden glow: Castle Pines Golf Club combines natural beauty with brilliant design.**

Country Club of Castle Pines

Castle Rock, Colorado USA

This course was designed by Jack Nicklaus as a first-class course for residents of the exclusive estate home sites that are woven into the 5000 acre site of the Castle Pines Land Company development. For a brief history of the Castle Pines Land Company and the golf complex, which also includes the Castle Pines Golf Club course, see the immediately preceding course discussion, which features the brilliantly designed Castle Pines Golf Club course.

There is a lot of hillside play at the Country Club of Castle Pines, and this provides excitement, challenge, magnificent vistas and an altogether memorable golfing experience. The course starts out with a 544-yard par five. This a complex, but not inappropriate, starting hole and its green is bounded by a hillside with a very fine view of the course locale. The second hole is a par three that culminates in a green that is situated on a hillside. The third describes a dogleg left which is fairly well bunkered. Hole number four's green is located

Above: **The Country Club of Castle Pines hole number eight.** *Below:* **The seventeenth tee boxes, from the tenth tee.** *Above right:* **The first green at Castle Pines.** *Below right:* **The challenging second green.**

among the trees, with bunkers emplaced where they will add most to the challenge.

Hole number five, at 670 yards, is the longest hole on the course and is a driver's hole without a doubt. It describes a double dogleg, with some interesting fairway configuration. The sixth fairway fades to the left in its second half, leaving you with a carry over hazard to an obliquely placed green. Hole seven is a dogleg left that sets you up for hole eight.

The eighth is a shallow dogleg left featuring elevated tee boxes that look and feel like gunnery positions. Also featured here is an extremely challenging fairway whose contours are as beautiful as they are dangerous! Hole number nine is a double dogleg serpentine with its fair share of defenses.

Golfers at hole number ten tee off uphill to a dogleg left fairway having quite adequate defenses. The eleventh hole plays to a split fairway with hazard running through its cleft, and a green which is set obliquely. Hole number twelve is a par three which features a

hillside challenge; hole thirteen is a dogleg left that sets you up for another par three, the fourteenth hole.

Holes fifteen and sixteen get you limbered up with a chance to drive. Then, hole seventeen's elevated tee boxes challenge your depth and distance perception as you tee off for the green at this great, tree-framed par three. Not only that, but the views from the seventeenth tees—of the valley as it sweeps away from you to yet another mountain range—are inspiring.

Hole eighteen is a dogleg left that points you back to the clubhouse. The Country Club at Castle Pines provides a very fine round of golf in the scenic mountains of picturesque Colorado.

Below: A view of the fairway contouring of the eighth hole at Castle Pines. The vistas on this course are rare and beautiful. *Above opposite:* A look up from the eighth fairway to the rock-walled elevated tee boxes.

Hole	1	2	3	4	5	6	7	8	9	Out	
Championship	544	188	489	449	670	415	394	467	387	4003	
Regular	507	165	468	437	632	383	369	412	315	3688	
Middle	469	138	441	420	589	363	340	386	282	3428	
Forward	440	119	364	342	538	291	332	350	253	3029	
Par	5	3	4	4	5	4	4	4	4	37	
Hole	**10**	**11**	**12**	**13**	**14**	**15**	**16**	**17**	**18**	**In**	**Total**
Championship	411	572	168	433	191	462	551	144	363	3295	7298
Regular	390	540	140	406	181	419	511	142	341	3070	6758
Middle	368	514	119	381	157	419	511	142	302	2913	6341
Forward	327	452	94	356	88	374	435	129	235	2490	5519
Par	4	5	3	4	3	4	5	3	4	35	72

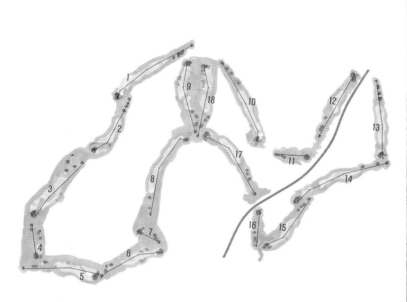

The Dallas Athletic Club (Blue Course)

Dallas, Texas USA

Jack Nicklaus won his first PGA championship here in 1963. In 1984, a severe winter caused the Board of Directors of The Dallas Athletic Club to decide that the course was due for renovation. The 30-year-old seed beds on the greens and the Bermuda grass fairways suffered a tremendous loss of grass. A *complete* renovation was decided upon–therefore, a course architect was needed. As the Dallas Athletic Club publicity release states, 'It was agreed that Jack Nicklaus would be the ideal choice, since he had won his first PGA championship on the course 30 years earlier and had already established himself as one of the great golf course architects in the world.'

One can assume that this was an enjoyable project for Jack–given his golfing career's connection with the course. This project marks the first time he has totally redesigned a course on which he won a major championship. He made his initial site visit in September of 1984. On 18 February 1985 construction began, and on 1 March 1986 the Blue Course had been successfully redesigned and was open once again for Dallas Athletic Club member play. This is a private club.

This is a 6710 yard course rated at par 72. A series of lakes divides the course laterally, and other lakes add interest elsewhere. You start off with par five hole number one, a tree-lined rightward arc. The green is set on a narrow

approach. Number two features a stream carry from the tees, and is a dogleg right, with a challenging fairway.

The third is another dogleg right, headed opposite hole two. It is the longest hole on the course at 553 yards. Trees line the fairway on the inside of its arc, and the green has a narrow approach, is bunkered at right front, and has a stream behind. Number four is a carry from the tees over a lake. The green is set into trees, has bunkers at right and left rear, and has the lake all along its front. It's a very challenging par three.

Hole number five is a sharp dogleg right, with a long carry from the tees over the opposite side of the lake we encountered at number

four. The fairway has trees along its inner bend, and another water carry is needed to get to the green, which has a bunker imbedded in its right side, and which is practically surrounded by water.

Golfers at hole six have to deal with a slope at the beginning of the fairway, and then face the challenge of a split level green, with a bunker at left front. The seventh is a par three lake carry to a split level green. Hole eight is a dogleg left with a multitude of bunkers and trees on its inner curve. The green is well-bunkered left and right.

The ninth's tree-lined fairway gives way to the arm of a lake, which must be carried to reach the split level green. Trees and a bunker

at left rear add excitement to an already considerable challenge. The tenth is a 510 yard straightaway, with trees near the tees to add interest. Just shy of midway down the tree-lined fairway are a couple of hummocks at left which should be taken into consideration. Trees to the right announce the end of the fairway and a substantial water carry to a complex fairway/green setup that hides the green–sandwiched between two bunkers–in the trees.

Hole number eleven features a long lake carry to a dogleg right, and another water carry to a green which is backed by a bunker and hillocks, and has a huge bunker at front right, and water elsewhere to the front and side. This green exists on the same island as do the tees for hole twelve, where you tee off over water to a fairway which has two bunkers left, and three bunkers right, which are strategically placed near its end. A minimal chipping fairway and the green can be reached by a carry over a shallow gulch. This is a split level setup, and should, combined with the angle of the green, make for a real test of ability.

Hole thirteen is a long tee shot to the fairway, which has a bunker at right, forcing most shots left. This presents the golfer with two left-lying obstacles in the form of hummocks. Trees lining the fairway on the left complete the defense there. The green is a split level target with a bunker on its left. The fourteenth is a par three water carry to a brief fairway/green setup. The green has bunkers, and water, at right and at left rear.

Hole fifteen is a shallow curve to the left.

Below left: **A view from the fairway of the eleventh green. Behind the hillocks shown here are the tees for the twelfth hole.** *Above left:* **Another view of the Blue Course. Trees, water and impeccable design—these are the marks of an aesthetically stimulating challenge.**

lined with trees and having a bunker at its midpoint on the left. A gunsight composed of slopes which intersect at mid-green makes this green a very difficult one to negotiate. Hole sixteen is a par three lake carry to a green which nestles in among the trees and has longitudinal bunkers left and right.

It's a long way from the back tee to the fairway of hole seventeen. Trees line this playing surface, and a serpentine hummock winds its way from the left to mid-fairway to cut into the left front of the green. This green approach is a dandy of a challenge, and one needs be ready for it.

The eighteenth features trees, bunkers, a

hummock—everything but water! Tee shots here must deal with a shallow ravine just before the fairway, and three big bunkers at left keep most shots tending to the right. The green approach has three bunkers which essentially form a beachhead, and a small hummock at left with a bunker behind it lie beyond these—all front the green. The green is therefore well guarded, with (additionally) a hummock at right rear and trees generally surrounding it on three sides.

It's a great golf course—and perhaps the PGA will look to the Dallas Athletic Club to host another championship here on this sparkling, championship quality course.

Hole	1	2	3	4	5	6	7	8	9	Out	
Gold	518	412	553	208	428	388	166	324	388	3385	
Blue	496	390	531	179	360	364	143	280	377	3120	
White	492	385	526	163	355	341	124	259	372	3017	
Red	467	332	500	136	324	281	103	247	351	2741	
Par	5	4	5	3	4	4	3	4	4	36	
Hole	10	11	12	13	14	15	16	17	18	In	Total
Gold	510	371	351	534	175	391	175	436	382	3325	6710
Blue	487	344	324	513	157	370	158	398	356	3107	6227
White	482	338	303	484	144	365	144	371	326	2957	5974
Red	461	275	283	442	122	337	117	317	268	2622	5363
Par	5	4	4	5	3	4	3	4	4	36	72

Desert Highlands Golf Club

Scottsdale, Arizona USA

The Desert Highlands Golf Club is situated at the foot of Pinnacle Peak, in the exquisitely beautiful desert environs of Scottsdale, Arizona. It is a private, 850-acre residential community with full golf and tennis facilities, plus other leisure time amenities. The tennis facility offers a choice of grass, clay or hard surfaces.

Jack Nicklaus' golf course designs for Desert Highlands include one 18 hole tournament course *and* an 18 hole putting course. Great care was taken to preserve the natural beauty and ecosystem of the desert in the building of this project. When Jack Nicklaus was making his plans for the two courses in 1982, he pledged, 'Insofar as possible, let's appreciate it as the place that it is.' Today, he is quoted in the Desert Highlands brochure as saying, 'I believe we succeeded.'

The course design follows the old Scottish stratagem of following the existing terrain. Simple as it seems, it has the advantage of greatly facilitating environmental preservation efforts, and, of course, provides the classic Scottish sense of the unexpected in golf play. It is the sort of plan that requires a true mastery of touch—and a sure sense of golfing possibilities on the part of the course architect.

Where desert flora had to be moved to make way for the course design, the talents of Phil Hebets' Sonoran Desert Designs were enlisted to salvage the plants. Some 500 paloverde and ironwood trees were successfully relocated; more than 1000 saguaro cacti (ranging from 15 to 45 feet in height, and some as old as 200 years) were found new homes in gardens and home sites; and smaller

Above: Jack Nicklaus, course designer, sizes up a putt at Desert Highlands. *Below:* Sunrise over the eleventh hole—note the natural desert drywash at photo left. *At right:* The first hole, seen from above the tees.

cacti and such natural shrubs as brittlebrush, bursage and jojoba were transplanted as densely as two thousand to the acre. Also, in another step taken to boost nature conservation, Desert Highlands is irrigated with reclaimed waste water.

The putting course—inspired by the celebrated, but shorter, putting course at St Andrews, Scotland (which is indicatively nicknamed 'The Himalayas')—is the only 18 hole putting course in the Western Hemisphere. With varying pin and tee placements, there are many different levels of play to be had on this par 41 course.

The putting course itself extends 362.3 yards. That yardage includes five memorable par three holes, and of these, hole number four is a test of putting skill for any golfer. This hole is 46.7 yards of plummeting, slippery putting challenge—including three long tiers

and a pause under an elm tree off the putting surface. The scuttlebutt has it that, so far, just one ace has been scored on the putting course fourth.

Now that we've had a visit to the putting course, let's move on to the par 72 tournament course, which, due to its variable tee settings, stretches from 5082 yards at the front tees to 7099 yards at the 'Nicklaus' (championship) tees. This makes for a very satisfying selec-

tion of levels of play, with an average of four tee placements to choose from.

Hole number one features a tee shot from a granite grotto. This shot descends 125 feet to an undulating green that requires accuracy. Tee shots on the second hole must carry an expanse of desert to an island fairway. The green is tucked around behind a large bunker, and mounds protect the left periphery.

The third is a dogleg right with mounds to

the right, but an accurate drive should miss these. This is said to be the most challenging par four on the course. The green here is protected on its right front with a bunker, and on the left and behind with mounds. A challenge, indeed.

Hole number four, a demanding par three, features a goodly carry over desert vegetation and dry wash to a split level green with a bunker along its front, and deep hollows on its

Above: Desert Highlands is complete with native cactus and chaparral—as little of which has been relocated, for course construction, as is possible.

Below: The unparalleled putting course at Desert Highlands, inspired by the celebrated, but shorter, putting course at St Andrews, in Scotland.

At right: The sixteenth hole, seen from behind the tees. Note the tiered levels of the green, and the intermingling of both natural and man-made hazards.

left and rear. The fifth hole's tees are elevated 50 feet higher than the green, and the back tee is situated on a brushy slope such that golfers have to concentrate on accuracy as well as distance to reach the fairway, which presents its narrow end to the tees, and broadens to include mounds, bunkering and hollows to give you a 'run for the money.'

Hole six features two fairways that are split by an arroyo. The right fairway would seem at first to be easier than the undulating and heavily mounded left fairway, but when it comes time to go for the green, golfers on the right fairway find themselves confronted by a ridge of mounding. Any way you play it, this will be a challenge.

The seventh hole is a par three with a small, sloping green. Hole number eight tempts you with a long finger of fairway stretching toward the tees, but that long finger also invites your ball into a deep trench that cuts across the fairway—therefore, it may be better to try to carry the bunker that fronts the fairway's blunter, but less perilous, right portion. The green is well protected.

Hole nine plays uphill toward Pinnacle Peak, and that is an also apt nomenclature for this demanding three-shot hole. A 567-yard par five, features here are a hazard that cuts across the fairway just beyond the halfway point, and just beyond this, where the fairway cuts left, mounding at a strategic point

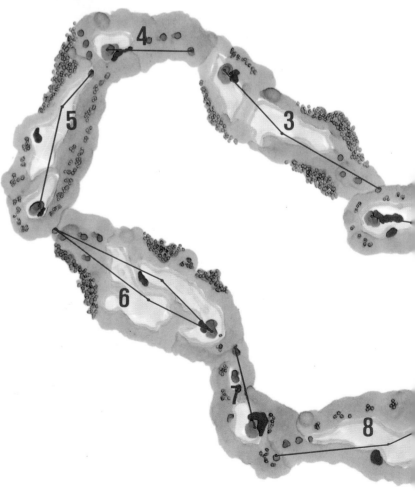

emphasizes accuracy on the green approach. The green itself has a bunker at left front and mounds and hollows on its periphery.

The tenth hole abuts the driving range and plays downhill. Its back tee box is a rocky nook at the foot of Pinnacle Peak, and its fairway is mounded and rolling. A dry wash guards the front of the split level green, and bunkers guard the rear. The eleventh is a double dogleg right, with a drywash across the fairway in two places, and an undulating green that demands accuracy.

The par three twelfth hole features tee settings that not only offer varying distances, but also varying angles of approach to a well-protected green that is the largest on the course. Hole number thirteen offers a choice of fairways, as did the sixth. This time, it's a very long carry over desert and mounds for the right-hand fairway, and an easier shot to the left fairway, with the liability that this route leaves you to face a shrub-filled natural wash on the green approach.

The fourteenth hole offers a beautiful vista—which serves to distract golfers at the tees. This hole is a dramatic dogleg left with a heavily contoured fairway having a 'bottleneck' green approach with lots of mounds

Above opposite: **Masterfully designed course defenses and choice desert vistas make the course at Desert Highlands something special.** *Below opposite:* **A young golfer and his instructor.**

and hollows adding protection for the terraced green. Hole fifteen is a 145 yard par three, with a green that is protected on its approach by hollows and bunkers, and has shrubbery and a rock outcropping at its rear. The sixteenth is the second of two par threes in a row, and features a distant, three-tiered green that steps away from the line of play. It could be a tricky one to play.

Hole number seventeen, at 570 yards the second-longest hole on the course, is a long

way downhill toward the green, with a heavily mounded green approach and a gang of bunkers fronting the green. It gets you ready for the eighteenth, which is not quite as long, but jogs left to a small, hidden, split level green that is surrounded by mounds and hollows.

This brings you back nearly to the clubhouse. It was from atop nearby Clubhouse Rock that Jack Nicklaus first surveyed the desert, in preparation for laying out this fine golf course.

Hole	1	2	3	4	5	6	7	8	9	Out	
Nicklaus	356	584	452	211	425	431	190	438	567	3654	
Back	303	489	401	177	406	416	137	398	529	3256	
Middle	285	484	368	150	373	382	107	375	487	3011	
Front	217	393	332	122	340	335	84	323	444	2590	
Par	4	5	4	3	4	4	3	4	5	36	
Hole	10	11	12	13	14	15	16	17	18	In	Total
Nicklaus	408	564	177	396	417	145	244	570	524	3445	7099
Back	363	546	175	348	372	131	225	537	492	3189	6445
Middle	295	508	138	318	346	105	198	494	448	2850	5861
Front	253	451	107	285	300	73	149	457	417	2492	5082
Par	4	5	3	4	4	3	3	5	5	36	72

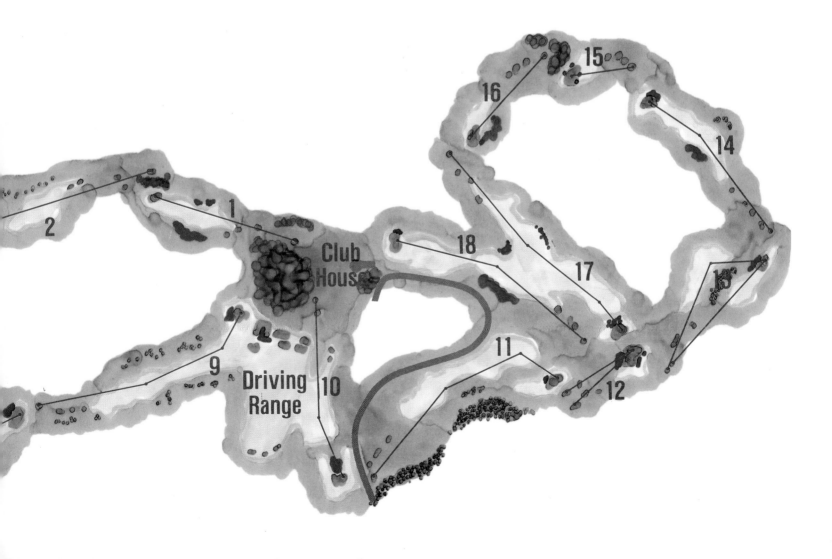

The Golf Club at Desert Mountain

Scottsdale, Arizona USA

The Golf Club at Desert Mountain is located near Scottsdale, in the ruggedly picturesque High Sonoran Desert. This area is lush with a variety of desert plants, including yucca, saguaro cacti, paloverde, ironwood and mesquite trees, and even junipers. Tan, coarse-grained granite forms natural sculptures that punctuate the already-impressive scenery.

This landscape is replete with winding arroyos that turn to gurgling streams in summer thunderstorms, and the desert's warm days and cool nights create an enchantment that has to be experienced to be fully appreciated.

The 8000-acre Desert Mountain complex is envisioned as a residential and recreational community for the coming century. Taliesin Associated Architects—founded by Frank Lloyd Wright—has created the master plan, which includes three 18-hole Jack Nicklaus-designed golf courses, clubhouses, proposed resorts, a professional office park and a village center for fine shops and other community services.

Says Jack Nicklaus, as quoted by a Desert Mountain brochure, 'Desert Mountain may be the finest golf complex in the United States.' The three courses—Renegade, Cochise and Geronimo—are entirely different and offer the utmost in playing challenge. Renegade and Cochise are currently open for play, while Geronimo is scheduled for completion either later this year, or in early 1990. Of these three courses, Cochise and Geronimo are strictly private—for members and their guests—while the Renegade course is available not only to members, but to non-member Desert Mountain property owners and resort guests.

Renegade is a completely new concept. It features a unique twin-flag, extended green system that allows for a variety of approaches to the pin and lets the expert and the average golfer play together and test their abilities equally.

Cochise has very smooth slopes and dramatic elevation changes. By contrast, the Geronimo plan calls for steep banks and elevation changes across and around ravines and plateaus. Therefore, Cochise is the 'soft-looking' course, and Geronimo is the 'hard looking' course, but both will test your skill at a variety of levels of play.

Again, a word from Jack Nicklaus, as quoted in a Desert Mountain brochure—'It's been my goal to preserve the natural environment so you can experience the beautiful and inspiring scenery while at the same time playing a challenging round of golf.'

These latter two courses are located in an area of exquisite scenery, with views of mountains, rock outcroppings and desert vegetation. Also, encompassing the whole area of

Above: **Jack Nicklaus, designer of this three-course facility.** *At right:* **The Renegade at Desert Mountain twelfth, which plays as a par three *or* a par four.**

these two courses is a 600 acre 'golf park' botanical preserve, with an extremely wide variety of high Sonoran desert plants and trees—planned to include nature walks and appropriate identification and information of the desert growth, as is done in arboretums.

Desert Mountain has a sophisticated and comprehensive transplantation program to relocate vegetation to a central nursery during construction. When land has to be cleared to make way for a part of the development, Jeff Hoffman—the superintendent for Hubbs Brothers Landscaping—and his crew walk the proposed site for days, literally tagging everything for transplantation, from the largest to the smallest of the existing flora.

Plants are carefully uprooted, given appropriate trimming and transported to the nurs-

ery for care until they are ready for transplanting at appropriate locales on the Desert Mountain site. Desert Mountain's management is so committed to preservation of the desert that even boulders are transported to the storehouse for future 'replanting' on the development site.

Jack Nicklaus' positive approach to conservation makes these efforts much easier. If a rock outcropping would interfere with a hole

design, Jack finds another place to put the hole, for the sake of saving the outcropping and for the sake of the course's honest playability.

Let's go for a brief tour of the two extant courses at Desert Mountain—and these will surely whet your appetite to know more about the unfinished Geronimo course. First, we'll consider the Renegade course, which plays around—and partially through—the planned residential development.

With two flag settings on the same green—or, in the case of five holes, on separate greens—and a number of tee settings besides, yardages on this course range from 5136 to 7515 yards, offering every imaginable skill level a challenging round of play. Hole number one has two fairways, both of which are lined with hills, and at their midpoints, with bunkering. The right fairway will let you avoid the 'hallway of bunkers' effect of the left, yet it leaves you with a carry over a wall of bunkers on your approach to either of the two pins—which, as we have said, are a unique feature of every hole on this challenging course.

The second hole plays down a wide fairway with a bunker set nearly in its middle—some will lay up short, some will chance the carry. The two-pin green wraps around a deep bunker from behind, and uneven ground completes the peripheral protection. That back pin will present a real challenge.

Hole three is a slight dogleg right, with a front pin that is protected by a bunker at left front and hills on either side and behind, and the back pin necessitates a carry over desert land to a separate green having bunkers behind. The par three fourth hole features a lake carry to an elongated and well-bunkered green. Of course, that back pin is just a bit harder to reach.

Hole number five is a driving hole that leads you to a fascinating challenge: desert flora to one side makes that shot to the green of the front pin truly a matter of accuracy, while the bunker-lined approach to the back green and pin rhymes in a limerick of black humor with the contouring behind the pin. The par three sixth plays to an hourglass-shaped green with a narrow, bunker-protected 'waist.' For the front pin, it's a matter of 'too far is real trouble,' and for the back pin, it's a carry over same, with the added caveat that too far here will land you in the desert.

Hole number seven features a carry over a flotilla of bunkers halfway down, making the back pin the object of a pin-point carry between them and the right-lying bunker on the green approach. Greenery behind the green itself assures your probable concentration on accuracy here. The front pin is a bit more accessible—but not by much.

The eighth is a dogleg left, with shrubs and small hills on the right to provide hazards on that perimeter, and a wide, shallow front green. The back green lies across a deep desert wash. The ninth hole builds with a fine momentum, down a fairway split with bunkers on the respective green approaches, and provides an uncomfortably crafty arrangement of contouring and bunkers to protect the respective greens. The back pin has, in addition to this, a row of trees on the left periphery of its approach.

Hole ten is lined on both sides with greenery, and plays along a fairway that has a vicious long line of bunkers to the right of most probable landing spots. It also, at this point, presents you with a choice: the fairway has a 'calf' to its left here, which allows closer access—at the cost of an additional stroke—to the front pin. The other choice is to try to carry from the primary fairway, over the evenly-spaced bunkers that front the green that is shared by both the front and back pins. Behind the green is a small mountain range of gentle mounding.

The eleventh is a dogleg right, with a bunker perched dead center in the fairway, at the foot of a ridge that runs completely across the green approach. The green itself is irregularly shaped, and is fronted by a wide bunker. Either pin on this hole represents a worthy achievement.

Hole number twelve is a par three that also plays as a par four from alternate tees. There is a lake-and-bunkers carry off the tees here, with a split level green changing the elevation between the front and back pins, and a small bunker in the middle of the green at the elevation change. The thirteenth hole features a long carry from tees to fairway, and has a bunker placed in the most challenging spot imaginable for shots to the fairway. This hole is a dogleg right, and has a split-level, ell-shaped

green that puts the back pin behind a deep bunker.

Hole fourteen is a par three that plays to a split level green that is well-bunkered in front and has a steep hillside behind. Hole fifteen, a dogleg right, plays to an island fairway with strategically placed bunkers. A rift in the fairway increases the challenge, and trees and contouring complicate the green approach. The far pin, with its narrow green approach, is additionally guarded with bunkers and desert.

The sixteenth is a par three that features a carry over a desert wash that fronts the green. The split level green further includes a mid-green bunker that protects the back pin—for a real challenge there. Hillocks back the green, especially behind the front pin—beware of overflights.

Hole number seventeen has two fairways. The left-lying fairway allows golfers to avoid a longer carry over the desert and contouring that front the right fairway. The tradeoff is that greenery blocks the way for a possible stroke-saving shot from the left fairway toward the green. The green, backed against the hillside, has trees on the left—on the side of the front pin—and a bunker fronting the back pin, on the right.

The eighteenth hole is a 425 yard par four that is a dogleg right, with a bunker on the inside of its knee, and a ridge along the left side of the fairway. The green is a three-lobed

affair with bunkers tucked into each of its inner curves. With a surrounding steep hillside to complement the bunkering, either pin setting will provide you with the challenge to complete a great round of golf.

Let's now move on to the Cochise course, which opened in November of 1987. After a luncheon for members and guests, Jack Nicklaus played the first round on the new course, accompanied by 1987 US Amateur champion Bill Mayfair. Their round of golf was witnessed by approximately 1000 people. The event was followed by cocktails and dinner.

On November 13 a special luncheon was held for the ladies—including members,

The Renegade Course at Desert Mountain

Hole	1	2	3	4	5	6	7	8	9	Out	
Professional Gold	455	438	449	230	531	199	398	480	576	3756	
Championship Blue	421	405	418	207	510	173	359	459	520	3472	
Regulation White	387	357	406	177	486	160	345	400	504	3222	
Forward Red	328	348	366	173	469	134	325	273	478	2894	
Par	4	4	4	3	5	3	4	4	5	36	
Hole	10	11	12	13	14	15	16	17	18	In	Total
Professional Gold	586	407	288	474	236	608	167	568	425	3759	7515
Championship Blue	570	368	186	459	200	592	151	539	403	3468	6940
Regulation White	498	344	164	417	185	561	136	508	359	3172	6394
Forward Red	442	312	118	362	147	462	107	428	303	2681	5575
Par	5	4	4/3	4	3	5	3	5	4	36/37	73/72

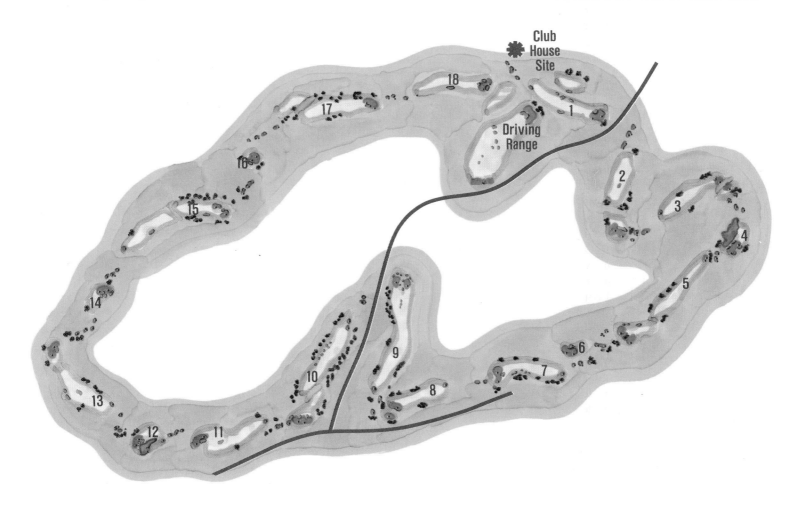

Above: **The seventh and fifteenth greens (left and right) of Cochise at Desert Mountain. Cochise is a comparatively soft course, but is not to be taken lightly, despite its graceful contours.**

members' wives and their guests. A discussion on the construction and exterior design of southwestern homes, and a fashion show by Capriccio, rounded out the afternoon. Throughout the week, the Cochise course was open for play, and special provision for guest play was made.

The Cochise opening events concluded with a tournament for members and guests on the Cochise and Renegade courses. The two-person teams played one round on each championship course. The internationally known golf instructor Jim Flick, director of golf instruction at Desert Mountain, and Richard Brain, Desert Mountain's international golf coordinator, were teamed with director of golf Dick Hyland for advice and instruction throughout the tournament. On Sunday, November 10, an awards ceremony was held at the Cochise-Geronimo Clubhouse, after which cocktails and hors d'oeuvres were served.

Cochise has very large, very deep features, but its slopes are gentle, making for relatively easy maintenance. It is a strategic player's course, and has rolling landscape, deep ravines and dramatic rock formations to make it even more stimulating and challenging. It is a truly beautiful course.

With distances stretching from 7045 to 5246 yards depending on your level of play, this is a course to challenge golfers of any ability. The following is a hole-by-hole tour of

this magnificent course. The fairway at hole number one features a change of elevation, and an island which contains a bunker and some greenery—which presents an added impetus for a long carry. The green has a narrow approach with a large bunker to the left front.

Hole number two is a par three which plays across desert to a green nestled among granite outcroppings, with bunkers at right front and right rear. The third hole is a long dogleg right, lined with contouring and greenery, with a long, narrow, slope-fronted green set off to the right. One bunker guards the rear of the green.

The fourth hole is a par five dogleg left, with contouring on its outer perimeter, and with bunkers set strategically on its inner curve. The small, split level green has a bunker out in front and containment grass bunkers behind.

The fifth plays along a two-pronged fairway, the right prong of which reaches closer to the tees and has a massive bunker halfway down its left edge, just where the leading edge of the left prong arrives. Those electing to drive to the left prong, with its longer carry, must also beware of this huge bunker, but will be rewarded with shorter access to the split level green over a bunker at left front, with shrubbery to the left. For those who take the right prong all the way, its sharp bend to the left could lead unthinking shots into the bushes or a rock formation. Either way, it's a challenge.

Hole number six, with alternate greens, also features a long shot from the back tees,

and a carry over rock formations from the front tees. The sharp right curve of the fairway tucks the right front green behind a big bunker winding through another clump of rocks, while the sharply curving front green approach is further guarded by rocks. The front green is heavily contoured on its right periphery, and has a bunker at left. The punch bowl back green—atop a granite-studded hill—features a shaver of a carry over rocks, bunkers and desert to capture this prize that tests those with advanced skills.

The par three seventh—with a backdrop of mountain ranges and the city below—is the second longest par three on the course and has a long carry from the back tees. The lake that surrounds the green could encourage some players to lay up on the fairway before carrying the water, but the valiant will go for the split level green from the tees. Bunkers and rock formations further increase the beauty—and the challenge—of this fabulous hole, that shares its island green with the fifteenth hole.

The eighth, a par five, is the longest hole on the course, and is a driver's delight, with a two-part fairway that is luxuriously long, but comes to a challenge with the third shot—to the deep, narrow, and slightly elevated green.

The ninth is a dogleg left, with a long carry from the fairway to the green, which itself has one bunker out front, bunkers to the right, a bunker to the left and rocks at right behind. The subtle angles of this hole will test your abilities.

Hole ten is a dogleg left, with a bunker carry from the tees. Across the fairway from the bunkering are smaller bunkers. A narrow green approach, a change of elevation and a split level green all add to the challenge here. The eleventh hole is a par three thriller, with tee shots requiring a carry not only over extensive bunkering, but rock formations as well. Better make sure your feet are planted right before you stroke here. The green is protected by rocks and bunkers behind and to the sides, as well.

Hole twelve is a long dogleg right, with a green approach that hooks sharply and includes a carry over desert rough. Those seeking to shave strokes on this par five face the challenge of a desert wash cutting across the fairway in front of the green and a carry over rock formations and a bunker that defines the right end of the green. Shrubbery completes the defensive scenario here.

The thirteenth, a par three from a hilltop to two alternate greens below, features obstructions by way of greenery and rocks en route. Hole number fourteen is a driving hole that plays along a serpentine fairway with bunkers placed strategically along its left, and a sharply sloping green with contouring on both sides and behind.

The fifteenth is a 548-yard par five from the

back tees. Golfers drive to a wide fairway that nevertheless offers a test of accuracy at the very first, with a deep bunker set mid-fairway in the way of tee shots, and further obstruction by way of an intruding rock on the left near the green approach. The green approach itself features a water carry to an island green set in a lake on the same island as the number seven green. Here again, bunkers, rocks, shrubs and the water present a defense for this multi-level green. It is a truly *beautiful* challenge.

Hole number sixteen plays to a fairway with a large granite outcropping directly in its center. The green approach features a carry over desert rough, rocks to the right and a large bunker—which complements the inside curve of the green itself—to the left. A deep grass bunker behind, and a change of elevation in the green itself, further this test of golfing skill.

The seventeenth hole, a par three, has an obstructing rock formation at the right of the mouth of its fairway, and trees along the right serve to create tension, in concert with the large bunker that protects the exposed face of the green, which curves right. This is a multi-level playing surface, with grass bunkers and rocks behind it. It is an extremely challenging par three.

The eighteenth hole has a very long carry from the tees to the fairway, and a rock formation splits the mouth of the fairway—on the right is a large bunker and trees, but this route offers the possibility of getting greater distance than on the relatively clear, but fading, area left of the rocks. The fairway terminates, then begins again, with an irregular segment that has bunkers and greenery along its right perimeter. The green is small and shallow, with a narrow waist. A ledge of solid rock, fronted by a large bunker, forms a natural wall behind it, and a massive bunker lies off to the left. This is a worthy and challenging target to cap a magnificent test of golf.

As we have said, the steeper and more severe-looking Geronimo course is due to open in the near future. We do have some tantalizing information on this highly anticipated course, however. It is said to be 7364 yards from the professional tees, 6988 from the back tees, 6375 yards from the middle tees and 5833 yards from the front tees. Golfers can look forward with excitement to its completion.

At left: **Another view of the seventh and fifteenth greens of Cochise.** *Below right:* **A Desert Mountain sunset.** *At right:* **Jack Nicklaus at Desert Mountain: envisioning the completed Geronimo course?**

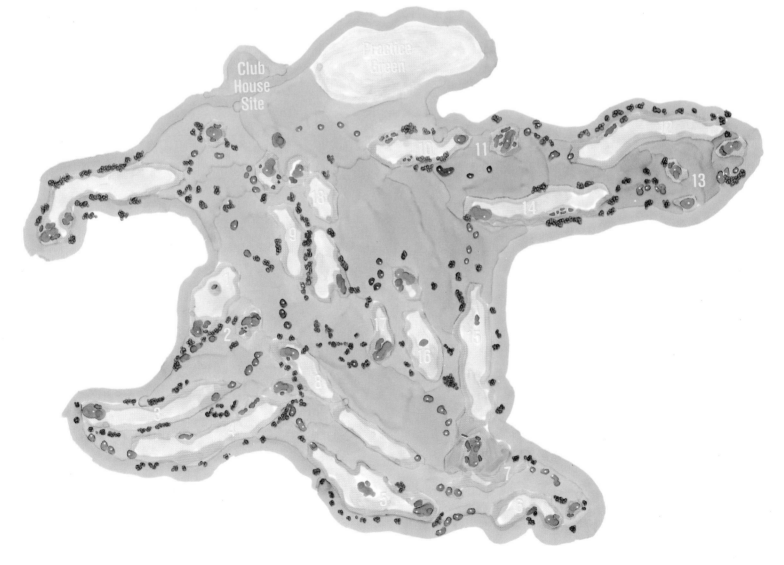

Cochise at Desert Mountain

Hole	1	2	3	4	5	6	7	8	9	Out	
Professional	397	191	475	546	448	385	215	569	411	3610	
Championship	390	181	457	525	408	331	194	546	385	3417	
Regular	345	141	426	483	394	295	178	517	351	3130	
Forward	284	107	375	442	353	259	146	428	300	2694	
Par	4	3	4	5	4	4	3	5	4	36	
Hole	10	11	12	13	14	15	16	17	18	In	Total
Professional	424	180	511	143	450	548	413	225	541	3435	7045
Championship	404	175	500	140	434	543	402	203	531	3323	6740
Regular	317	125	471	108	142	484	353	182	472	2924	6054
Forward	275	85	405	99	392	458	312	156	419	2601	5295
Par	4	3	5	3	4	5	4	3	5	36	72

Elk River Club

Banner Elk, North Carolina USA

The Elk River development is a private residential club of premier quality. The Elk River Clubhouse has a large pro shop, indoor golf instruction facility, men's and women's locker rooms and card rooms, and a golfers' grill. Construction of the main dining and social clubhouse is slated for completion this year (1989).

Adjacent to the clubhouse is the Tennis Center, which offers the finest facilities, including four outdoor courts, indoor courts, and other playing arenas, including a racquetball court. The Elk River Saddle Club consists of a full professional staff, modern stable, riding ring, jump course and several miles of riding trails. A 30-acre fenced pasture and paddock area adjoins the stable.

The private Elk River Airport is located on the premises. Its 4600-foot runway is capable of handling corporate jets and other private aircraft. Electronics here include a non-directional radio beacon and Unicom. The airport is available to members only.

Elk River offers a mixture of residential sites–both full home site plots from one to five acres, and condominiums. Electrical, telephone and television cables are run underground, to enhance the aesthetic appeal of this complex.

Our central concern here is, of course, the superb 18 hole championship golf course which was designed by Jack Nicklaus. Not only has the Nicklaus organization designed this course, the firm has a continuing involvement with the course insofar as maintenance, club operations and public relations are concerned. In addition, the Nicklaus family also maintains a residence at Elk River!

The 7000 yard course lies in the scenic Elk River Valley, and has been designed to harmonize with, and utilize as part of its design, this glorious natural setting. Offering challenge and enjoyment for all levels of golfing skill, this course offers four or five tee areas for each hole. Tees and greens are bent grass.

Construction began in spring of 1982, and play began in the summer of 1984. Like a living blanket on the beautiful rolling mountains of North Carolina, the many species of deciduous trees native to the area provide a seasonal pageant of rare charm. Embodying as it does all the elements of its superb natural setting, the Elk River Club course is considered by many to be one of golf's most beautiful and intriguing layouts. The following is a hole-by-hole description of this excellent new golf course.

Hole one is a dogleg left with bunkers on the outside of its bend. These bunkers are set to catch a variety of approach shots, and the green approach itself is squeezed from the left and right with bunkers. The second hole features a stream carry off the tees to a long, shallow dogleg right. Then it's another stream carry from the fairway to the green, which sits in a cul-de-sac of trees.

Hole number three, a par three, features a green which has bunkers at left rear, right rear and right side. The fourth is a long curve to the right having a serpentine fairway with

Below: **Elk River's second green—a stream separates it from the fairway.** *At right:* **Hole seventeen. Note the strategic bunker between the pond and the green.**

bunkers hidden among its curves, and a well-bunkered green. Hole number five is a very long reach from the back tee to the fairway. At the green approach, bunkers lie left, in the crook of the fairway neck—as if homing in on the green, which itself has a bunker at left.

Par three hole six features a carry over a stream and a monstrous bunker to an abbreviated fairway/green setup. The green is bunkered on both sides, and these bunkers are quite cannily placed. Hole seven is a long, shallow dogleg right, with a stream carry to a green which is surrounded by trees on three sides and has a bunker at left rear.

The eighth is a dogleg right with a carry over the Elk River off the tees. The fairway bulges to the right, where it pushes into a lake. Then a long lake carry is necessary to reach the green, which has one bunker out front, on the lake, and four all along its rear. It's possible to play this one safer, by going longer on the other side and aiming for the nubbin of fairway on the green side–just an instance of how wide a range of capabilities this course will allow.

The ninth hole is the second longest on the course, at 553 yards, and it gives you your money's worth. The back tee shoots through a row of trees to a fairway which is split by an access road. The carry to the second half comes close to the lake arm to the right, and then the carry to the green involves the Elk River and an islet. The green fronts on the river, is backed by trees and has one bunker on its left.

Hole ten is a driving hole. Shots from the back tee carry over the Elk River and pass perilously close to the copse of trees on the right. A lake that starts at midway on the long fairway will add interest on the left, and the narrow approach to the green has a bunker on its left, fronting the left of the green.

The eleventh hole, a par three, plays to an equal-sized fairway/green combination. The green is shaped somewhat like a flattened valentine set sideways, with a bunker on each of its three indented sides, and trees to the right rear. Hole number twelve is the longest on the course at 555 yards. It forms a dogleg left to a green which is canted even more sharply left behind a double row of bunkers.

Hole	1	2	3	4	5	6	7	8	9	Out	
Championship Blue	376	392	175	326	467	180	512	360	553	3341	
Member's White	359	374	161	301	394	164	492	345	502	3092	
Senior's Yellow	321	325	121	287	378	151	427	319	463	2792	
Women's Red	292	305	96	237	318	140	398	278	442	2506	
Par	4	4	3	4	4	3	5	4	5	36	
Hole	10	11	12	13	14	15	16	17	18	In	Total
Championship Blue	474	212	555	394	429	497	369	161	414	3505	6846
Member's White	439	195	491	343	388	480	349	140	377	3202	6294
Senior's Yellow	402	172	453	309	343	464	307	129	341	2920	5712
Women's Red	382	119	433	285	321	379	281	116	320	2636	5142
Par	4	3	5	4	4	5	4	3	4	36	72

Below left: **Hole fifteen, as viewed from the opposite bank of a tributary of the Elk River. The Elk River flows through the midst of the course, and passes by the fifteenth again on the left side of its green.** *Above:* **A vista down an Elk River Golf Course fairway. Compare with the hole map.**

Those bunkers on the right just before the green approach should be paid attention to, and the bunker at right rear of the rather narrow green completes the scenario here.

The thirteenth hole is a carry over rough from the last tee to a serpentine fairway. The green here has a prominent bunker on its left. The fourteenth is another moderate hole, again with a back-tee carry over rough to a fairway having a bunker to its right early on. The green has bunkers on its right and rear, and also at rear, a small stream bed.

Hole fifteen features a long tee carry—over two access roads and a tributary of the Elk River—and has to shave by just to the right of a grove of trees to a dogleg right fairway. Bunkers lie to the left of the fairway a little too early to be a factor unless you hook or slice your ball. The green hooks sharply to the right, and is bunkered on its right and left. A bunker protects the green approach from the right.

Hole sixteen describes a shallow curve to the right, and trees occupy the inside of its curve: opposite these, a row of three bunkers guard the right side of the fairway. A stream flows all along the left side of this hole. The approach to the green has a bunker cutting into it from the right, and the green itself has a tributary of the Elk River on its right, rear and left.

The seventeenth is a par three buildup to the eighteenth. The back tee on seventeen has a long carry to the green, including a lake, and a bunker lying in the ball flight path between the green and the lake. Hole number eighteen carries over rough and an access road to a fairway having a tributary of the Elk River all along its right. You must carry over the Elk River itself to reach the fragment of fairway/green setup on the other side. This fairway fragment leads to a pinched green approach with bunkers on both sides. A small bunker resides behind the green itself. The Elk River Club course offers 18 holes of superb golfing for players of all capabilities.

English Turn Golf & Country Club

New Orleans, Louisiana USA

The English Turn Golf & Country Club has, as of this year (1989), become the new home of the USF&G Classic, a prestigious PGA tour event that was hitherto known as the Greater New Orleans Open.

On the West Bank of the historic Mississippi, within fifteen minutes of downtown New Orleans, the Jack Nicklaus Development Corporation, in conjunction with USF&G Insurance and Classic Properties of New Orleans, has built one of the proudest additions to the roster of fine American golf and country clubs in the land.

The English Turn Golf & Country Club is situated in magnificent scenery, and the fine new 18 hole golf course was specifically designed to host the USF&G Classic, an event which is nationally aired on NBC-TV, and which purse has grown in recent years to $750,000.

The successful association of USF&G Insurance with this major golfing event led to a determination on the part of the insurance company to create an exceptional environment for the tournament, and thus USF&G was committed to establishing English Turn as one of the best tournament golf facilities in the US.

Though designed for the USF&G Classic, English Turn also features four sets of tees to provide a challenge for not only the tournament player, but for players at all levels, as well. The course features spectator areas and exciting fairway contours seldom seen in the area. The course is entirely surrounded by water, and this enhances both the challenge to players and the aesthetic qualities of this already beautiful locale.

Indeed, Jack Nicklaus himself made the statement, in the English Turn Golf & Country Club brochure, that 'I want the golf course and the country club at English Turn to incorporate the best ideas I've seen all over this country and the world—and then go a step further.' This dictum is followed through in style—as is indicated by the clubhouse, which is an exquisite replication of an Old New Orleans mansion, and is composed of 43,000 square feet of first-class social, sporting and recreational facilities. Full tennis and swimming facilities are provided, with full amenities, just as you enter the parking area.

Nowhere is this dedication to excellence

seen more clearly than in the layout of the magnificent golf course at English Turn Golf & Country Club. Water figures prominently in the way this course plays; it is surrounded with a channel that originates in a lake that is seen from the clubhouse, and goes on to form various lagoons here and there in its course around the layout, and ends, having come almost full circle, at the gate house near the parking complex. Ponds dotted here and there add water play in addition to the surrounding channel. The following is a hole-by-hole description of this exciting course.

Hole one is a 388 yard par four, with a water carry from the back tee. It forms a dogleg right, with a huge bunker guarding the majority of the front of the green, and water all along the hole, to the left. The second hole also features a water carry from the back tee.

Hole	1	2	3	4	5	6	7	8	9	Out	
Gold	388	525	190	345	455	548	442	172	363	3428	
Blue	366	498	175	310	430	529	420	140	340	3208	
White	346	478	150	295	400	486	388	118	326	2987	
Red	291	433	120	278	353	414	340	92	270	2591	
Par	4	5	3	4	4	5	4	3	4	36	
Hole	**10**	**11**	**12**	**13**	**14**	**15**	**16**	**17**	**18**	**In**	**Total**
Gold	417	530	150	373	456	530	402	213	463	3534	6962
Blue	380	506	133	360	425	510	370	190	440	3314	6522
White	365	470	110	343	409	496	350	176	424	3143	6130
Red	300	438	95	310	362	426	320	155	360	2766	5357
Par	4	5	3	4	4	5	4	3	4	36	72

The fairway here has, between it and the water all along its left, a vast longitudinal waste bunker, which creates tension for shots to the green—which hooks left, toward the water.

Hole three is a sharpshooter's par three. The green here is all but engulfed by a huge bunker which curls from halfway down the left of the fairway to the middle of the front of the green by way of the rear and right sides. A little pot bunker is set at left front of the green, as well.

The fourth's fairway is protected by a large lateral waste bunker. The back tee has a water carry to the fairway, and then *all* second shots have a water carry to the green. Hole five's tees have to deal with the incursion to the line of flight of the tip of a lagoon. The fairway is a contoured challenge, and should prove a enough of a change of pace to gear one up for the sixth hole.

The sixth hole features a water carry from the back tee, and a well-bunkered, contoured fairway leading up to a green which has a pond cutting into the approach from the right. Tee shots on the seventh are water carries for all but the front tee. The entire fairway and green here have a single longitudinal waste bunker to the left, on the other side of which lies the channel. The second shot is to a green guarded by mounds and formal bunkers, making club selection difficult.

Hole eight is a worthy par three, with tee shots going for a green which basically is set on a peninsula in the channel. Also, the back tee has a long water carry. Hole number nine is another water carry from the back tee, another full-length waste bunker on the left, and a green which has one small bunker on its left and a pond on its right.

Hole ten is a serpentine contest with contours and water all along the left, bunkers to the right and water carries to the well-trapped green. The eleventh hole plays directly across the course, giving the back tee a water carry over a pond instead of the channel. At 530 yards, eleven shares with hole fifteen the distinction of being the longest on the course. The channel accompanies the fairway on its right side now, and this long, left curve has a split fairway toward the end, with water still a factor on the right.

Hole twelve is a short par three with water all along its right. The green features severe undulations for adventuresome putting. Another dogleg right, hole thirteen has water, sand and grass bunkers all along its right. The back tee of hole fourteen plays across a pond. The fairway and green here are contoured, with the green a replica of the eighteenth green at Muirfield in Scotland. Water forms a second perimeter beyond the cart path.

The fifteenth plays with water very close on the right. Its green is set on an island off to the right in a lagoon, making this par five a real challenge to the player electing to try to reach the green in two shots. Hole number sixteen plays across the course. It has a waste bunker at right, and a formal bunker in front of the green.

Seventeen's tees are all situated on a peninsula in the lagoon, and have to carry across to a split fairway, though many will go straightaway for the green on this par three. A fully adequate formal bunker guards the green on the approach, and a smaller bunker balances this on the right side of the green's 'neck.'

Hole number eighteen is a magnificently satisfying conclusion to eighteen holes of golf at one of the finest golf complexes in the country. The back tee here is situated on an island, and the front tees have water to their left. The fairway has—in addition to a channel, and then a lake, to its left—a full-length waste bunker which transitions to formal bunkers that surround the green. Opposing the sand and water on the left side are five pot bunkers on the right side. This hole will not be conquered easily, but it'll be a great contest.

Glen Abbey Golf Club

Oakville, Ontario Canada

Glen Abbey is Canada's first public golf club to be specifically designed for major tournaments, with the spectator very much in mind. Jack Nicklaus, the renowned golfer and course designer, is quoted in Glen Abbey's *Pocket Pro* magazine and course guide as saying 'The idea was to build a championship golf course, a tough but fair golf course, but most of all an easily viewable golf course.'

This has been admirably accomplished, with Glen Abbey having celebrated its 10th year of hosting the Canadian Open Golf Championship. At Glen Abbey, the spectator mounds that have been built on the course come into play on several of the holes, as do the four lakes and Sixteen Mile Creek, not to mention such other spectacular defenses as steep canyon walls and magnificent trees.

Glen Abbey was originally a large country estate. When its owner died, he bequeathed it to a group of Jesuit priests for use as a retreat. After several years, the Jesuits left the estate, as it was too large to be properly taken care of. A group of Oakville businessmen purchased the property and turned it into the Upper Canada Golf & Country Club. It then became the Clearstream Golf & Country Club, and finally, it was renamed Glen Abbey.

The Jesuits left their mark on the property, in the form of the old stone building that is now the Royal Canadian Golf Association Headquarters, and the figure of the Jesuit monk who is shown swinging a golf club in the club logo.

Being the host for the Canadian Open has earned Glen Abbey a reputation as a good tournament course, and many corporate tournaments are held here. The Glen Abbey Clubhouse is an unusually striking tri-level structure with a central spiral staircase adjoining various accommodations for receptions, dinners and business meetings. The Jack Nicklaus Suite is ideal for small dinners, cocktail receptions and business meetings; its outside balconies offer a magnificent view of the course.

The main restaurant, with its full-length windows, offers an unobstructed view of the eighteenth hole and the lake, and is open for breakfast and lunch, Sunday brunch and, by special arrangement, can be reserved for receptions, dinner dances and other private

functions. The Glen Abbey Room is a large private banquet facility that is used by the media for interviews and coverage of the Canadian Open, and can be used for private seminars, receptions and other events. The cocktail lounge has full-length windows and indoor plants, and has access to an attractive outdoor patio.

In addition to this, 'The Champions' Club' allows you to unwind after a challenging round of golf. Full locker room and whirlpool bath, plus a luxuriant private lounge and secluded patio, are available for use in conjunction with small or large tournaments. A fully equipped pro shop, plus a full selection of golf clinics, lessons and workshops, complete the facilities at Glen Abbey.

The following is a hole-by-hole description of this fine course, which is one of the best in the great nation of Canada. Golfers at the first hole face a carry over bunkers through a hallway of trees to a landing spot on a narrow fairway that is guarded at right by a bunker. The tree-lined fairway leads to a green that is multi-level and heavily bunkered. Pin placement is also an important factor on this hole.

Hole number two has a tree and a bunker at left that make tee shots here a matter of

Below: **Golfers confront the second green approach— from the gold tees, a 414-yard par four.**

extreme accuracy. The landing area has trees to the left and bunkers, a mound, and trees to the right. The green approach is lowland, and the green is elevated, with one bunker at front left and one bunker at right rear. This is a good test of golf.

The third hole is a par three, with a long water carry to a wide, shallow green with large bunkers on both sides at rear and a smaller bunker at front center on the edge of the lake. Balls hit too hard will find an absolutely terrible lie behind the green, so just the right touch is required here. Players at the fourth hole have a water carry from the back tees. The landing area has trees to the right and bunkers to the left, and the approach has trees, a bunker and a mound to the right. The green has heavy bunkering on its left front, and trees to the right and behind.

Hole number five is a dogleg right that plays through a hallway of trees. A large oak on the right of the landing area presents an obstruction to be avoided—as does a tree farther down on the left, near the green approach. The green approach has trees on

both sides, and a bunker and a mound on the right. The green is tucked into a grove of trees, with bunkers on all sides leaving just the very center front open. Contouring makes the putting surface here very interesting.

The sixth hole has bunkers to the left of the landing area, and trees on both sides of the fairway all the way to the green approach. The green has a large spectator mound on its left and rear, and a large bunker on its right front. The seventh hole is a par three that plays into the wind. Trees to the right and left make this tee shot over a lake a rigorous test, and the bunkers on the left and right of the green add to the challenge here. Water is on the front and right of the green, and a spectator mound occupies the right rear. Trees lie over to the left. The lake here has swallowed a lot of balls.

Hole number eight has water and trees to the right of its tees, and the landing area has bunkers to its right and trees to the left. Two

Designed with players and public in mind. *At right:* Tournament play on the ninth. *Below:* A typical green: well-defended, and with ample spectator mounding.

These pages: An aerial view of the fourteenth hole. The lake to the left of the fairway is somewhat hidden, and the fourteenth tees are across the creek on the right.

bunkers are on the left front of the green, and a large single bunker is on the right front. A grass bunker guards the green approach on the right. Trees surround the green on three sides, and mounds are present to the right and rear. The green is narrow on the right side, so a shot to the middle or left is recommended.

The ninth hole has elevated tees, and the landing area is quite narrow, with trees on the left and mounds and bunkering on the right. The green approach is a carry over a lake to a small green with water on its front and right sides. A bunker at right front may serve as a saving grace for balls that would otherwise find the water. Trees at rear and left lie downhill. At this point, you might want to make a quick visit to the halfway house for refreshment, as the clubhouse is off-limits until you've completed your round.

The tenth hole is a water carry from the back tees. The landing spot has mounds and bunkers to the left, and trees to the right. The green approach has trees on both sides, and a bunker on the right. The green is long and narrow, and heads into a pocket of trees. On the right is a bunker, behind which is a stand of trees.

The eleventh hole takes you into the valley portion of this course. This hole is an extremely tough challenge, with a 220-yard carry from the back tee. Trees to the left and bunkers to the right make this long carry also a real test of accuracy—for those who can reach the fairway. The green approach is a carry over Sixteen Mile Creek to a small, narrow green having bunkers on both sides, trees behind and the creek along its front.

Hole number twelve is a par three that features a long carry over Sixteen Mile Creek to a green having bunkers all along its front, and a bunker and trees behind. The creek will swallow balls hit short, and still other underpowered hits will find a lie on the shore in front of the green; it's best to go long and to the right here.

The thirteenth hole has a creek carry from the tees, and the creek runs along the left of the fairway. Bunkers to the left of the landing area, and mounds farther down on the right, mingle with trees to form the defenses on that side of the fairway. Sixteen Mile Creek cuts across the green approach, in front of the extremely narrow green. A bunker in front adds sand to the dangers encountered by short hits here; long shots will find a very tough lie behind the green. Accuracy is a premium here.

Water in front of the tees and on both sides of the fairway is to be found at hole number fourteen. Fairway bunkers to the left of the landing area form a good target—and also a

At right: **Glen Abbey's third green. Its tees lie beyond the lake pictured here. It's a well-bunkered par three water carry that requires good shotmaking.**

serious hazard—for shots from the tees. The green is elevated and has a gully in its middle. This is a wonderful—and also dangerous—hole. Golfers at the par three fifteenth hole tee off across a valley to an elevated green. Large bunkers at left front and left rear add to the challenge here, as does the green tendency to roll toward the front.

The sixteenth hole is a tree-lined dogleg left. The green has bunkers on its left front and both sides in back. Overflights will find either the bunkers, the trees behind these or the hill that leads down to the thirteenth green. This is a hole for the brave, but prudent, golfer. Hole number seventeen presents a challenge to tee shots with a series of small bunkers on both sides of the fairway near the landing area. Those on the right will figure in a carry to the landing area on the middle-to-right side, near the trees there. This hole features a horseshoe-shaped green with trees to the left and rear, bunkers on its three exterior sides, and a bunker in the interior curve. Pin placement is crucial, given the shape and defenses of the green.

The eighteenth hole is a dogleg left, with heavy bunkering on either side of the landing area. Trees line the fairway from there on, and the green approach has a lake to the right that extends along the green. On the left and rear of the green are bunkers, and, additionally, a spectator mound lies to the left beyond the bunkers. Overflights produce extremely difficult lies, and shots to the left, sand—while those to the right mean lots of water. A stunning conclusion to eighteen holes of great golfing.

Hole	1	2	3	4	5	6	7	8	9	Out	
Gold	443	414	156	417	527	437	197	443	458	3482	
Blue	416	393	123	379	504	406	142	391	408	3162	
White	369	380	123	345	452	395	135	391	383	2973	
Par	4	4	3	4	5	4	3	4	4	35	
Hole	10	11	12	13	14	15	16	17	18	In	Total
Gold	435	452	487	529	426	141	516	434	500	3620	7102
Blue	489	439	182	515	367	122	466	421	455	3456	6618
White	435	426	152	481	330	115	452	390	448	3229	6202
Par	5	4	3	5	4	3	5	4	5	38	73

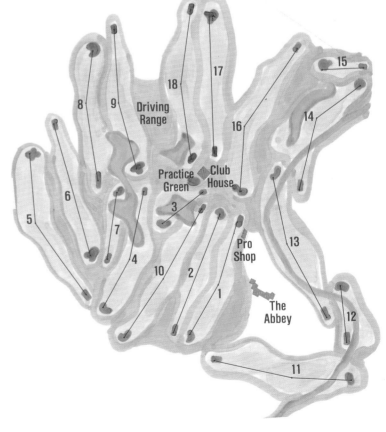

Below opposite: An aerial view of the eleventh hole, with fairway bunkers on the right, and the green across the creek. *Above left:* Teeing off from the blue tees at Glen Abbey's par three third hole. *Above:* The eighteenth green in tournament play. Note the spectator mounds, and the observation decks in the roof of the clubhouse. *Below:* Tournament play on a tree-lined hole. Glen Abbey has recently celebrated a decade of hosting the Canadian Open Golf Championship.

Grand Cypress Resort

Orlando, Florida USA

Grand Cypress Resort is owned and managed by the Dutch Institutional Holding Company (DIHC), based in Atlanta. The DIHC is the US based real estate entity of Pensionfund PGGM, the largest private pension fund in Holland, with managed assets of almost $16 billion.

Grand Cypress Resort is home to the Jack Nicklaus Academy of Golf, which, unlike many golf schools, allows students to practice their skills under actual playing conditions. The Academy's three-hole course with par three, par four and par five holes, plus varying pin and tee settings, provides as much variation as any student could desire.

Grand Cypress Resort has 45 holes of Jack Nicklaus-designed golf. The original 18 holes—the North and South nines—are referred to as 'The Grand Cypress,' and were recently voted into the *Golf Digest* 'Top 100 Courses in the United

Above: **A vista seen along a mounded fairway at the Old Course at Grand Cypress.** *Below:* **A misty view of the tenth green of the New Course at Grand Cypress.**

States.' Some years ago, a third nine was added to these, and is known as the East Nine. For the sake of tradition we'll begin our 18-hole tour with the North Nine and play onto the South Nine, and then we'll posit the East Nine as an alternate finish.

Hole number one on the North Nine of The Grand Cypress tees off to a rousing start beside a lake. The hole is a dogleg right with a tantalizing little chunk of fairway drifting off the prow of an obliquely-situated, oblong green that is sandwiched between two bunkers—'tantalizing' because it offers the tradeoff of an extra stroke for the ease of not having to make the necessary bunker carry to the green from the primary fairway.

The second hole plays along a serpentine fairway that has a bunker strategically placed to catch overflights from the tees. A lake is present along the left—from the midpoint of the fairway to the green—and a long bunker impinges on the green approach from the left. The green has yet another bunker at left rear.

Hole number three of the North Nine plays with a lake to its left, and is sandwiched with bunkers at its midpoint. The green hides behind a lobe of the lake—and also behind two bunkers, making for a carry that demands some valor. The fourth hole, a par three, has its tees backed up on a peninsula that extends into the same lake.

Hole five's mounded fairway leads you to a wineskin-shaped green which presents its neck first, and has bunkering on its right—just where miscalculated shots may find a resting place. The sixth hole is the longest of this nine, at 561 yards from the farthest tees. Its two-part fairway features a carry over rough and promises an interesting test of golf as you go for the irregular, obliquely-set green.

The seventh hole describes a rightward arc with a lake all along its interior curve, plus a long bunker set in same at its midpoint. 'Lake carry' is the word here, as the green hides itself behind the extreme end of the lake. Hole number eight is a par three that features a long, narrow green with longitudinal bunkers on either side.

The ninth hole has a serpentine fairway with a lake all along its left side, and has a lake carry on the green approach, with bunkers set in at the green's right rear and left rear.

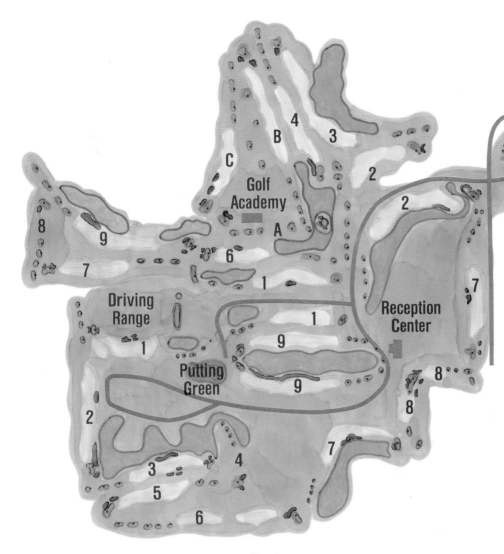

North

Hole	1	2	3	4	5	6	7	8	9	Total	
Gold	363	510	404	186	451	561	423	188	435	3521	
Blue	339	491	359	170	384	471	383	157	389	3143	
White	302	462	339	157	348	441	361	137	365	2912	
Red	287	410	307	119	301	402	345	108	350	2629	
Par	4	5	4	3	4	5	4	3	4	36	

South

Hole	1	2	3	4	5	6	7	8	9	Total	
Gold	352	553	158	428	364	570	432	183	463	3503	
Blue	327	513	145	383	310	539	404	169	416	3206	
White	315	478	105	351	295	506	367	141	384	2942	
Red	293	448	78	335	270	473	349	123	362	2731	
Par	4	5	3	4	4	5	4	3	4	36	

East

Hole	1	2	3	4	5	6	7	8	9	Total	
Gold	404	428	550	415	153	372	392	209	511	3434	
Blue	362	393	510	384	134	353	360	193	462	3151	
White	346	359	477	364	125	290	308	174	435	2878	
Red	269	309	401	283	99	275	247	150	394	2427	
Par	4	4	5	4	3	4	4	3	5	36	

Now we'll move on to the South Nine of this great course. The golfer at The Grand Cypress South hole one tees off with a pristine lake to his left. A serpentine fairway leads up to an obliquely-situated green that has bunkers all along its exposed face. This prepares you for hole two, which plays all along a lake, and features challenge after challenge. The valiant will want to shave strokes from their score-cards by making a lake carry on the sharply curving fairway; but beware—a large bunker defends the green approach in tandem with the lake. The green has bunkering on three sides, and the approach has to carry over the bunkering in front, as well as an arm of the lake. You'd better be on your game here.

The third hole is a par three that has a lake carry from all but the innermost tee, and from the back tee necessitates a carry down the length of the lake to the narrow chin of the green, which has bunkers set in on either side of its 'jaw,' and has the lake in front. Hole number four is a long dogleg left, the second half of which plays along a lake.

The fifth, a dogleg right, tees off with lakes in view—this could be a distraction, as golfers try to achieve a good landing on the serpentine fairway, which has a large, long bunker on its right, from the landing spot to the right face of the green. The green has three lobes, each with bunkering set in its inner curve.

The sixth hole is, at 570 yards, the longest on The Grand Cypress. It's a dogleg right with a cluster of bunkers set into the fairway near the likely landing spot for most tee shots. Two lakes off to the left provide distraction, and a longitudinal bunker guards the right of the green approach.

Hole number seven features a long carry off the tees, and bunkers intruding on the fairway from the right will make golfers want to consider their tee shots here very carefully. The green approach is narrow, and two bunkers to the left of an irregularly shaped green provide still more food for thought. A par three, hole eight has an island fairway and a very tricky wedge-shaped green, with heavy bunkering.

The ninth is a mirror image of its counterpart on the North Nine, with the astoundingly large longitudinal bunker on the inner curve of its fairway. This bunker fronts the lake, and extends all the way to the right side of the green. The green also has a bunker at rear.

These two nines are also known as the North and South nines of the Old Course at Grand Cypress—and we have one more nine to consider in this 27-hole complex. The East nine is not included when one speaks formally of 'The Grand Cypress,' but it presents its own special kind of challenge.

The Old Course at Grand Cypress' East Nine hole number one features a lake carry from the back tees, and its fairway detours around a big, right-lying bunker. The green is large and challenging. Hole number two is a dogleg right that plays to an unusual, crescent green with a crescent-shaped bunker at its rear. The third hole is a dogleg right that borders on a lake that will probably result in a stroke-shaving lake carry.

Holes four, five and six play around the three-hole course of the Jack Nicklaus Academy of Golf. Hole four's green is set on a stubby peninsula of land that projects into a lake, and has a large crescent bunker on the right of its green approach. The fifth hole is a par three, with its green on an island in the lake.

Hole six necessitates a lake carry from the tees, and overflights may cross the fairway only to find the large bunker on the right side there. The broad, shallow green has two bunkers behind it, and one strategically placed bunker on its right front. The seventh hole plays down a highly contoured fairway.

Hole eight is a par three that plays to an obliquely-set green that has a bunker on its left face. The ninth hole is a dogleg left that involves a huge left-lying bunker, two lakes and a green that is surrounded by bunkers.

Furthering the golfing challenge to be had at Grand Cypress Resort is The New Course at Grand Cypress, also designed by Jack Nicklaus. The New Course, while presenting a complement to the 27 holes of the Old Course, features steeper and more challenging bunkers and slopes. Various of its features pay homage to 'The Old Course' at St Andrews in Scotland, one of golfing's most revered courses.

Double greens, bridges and walls are some of the features that emphasize the Scottishness of the New Course at Grand Cypress. The course has 140 bunkers, ranging from small pot bunkers to far larger bunkers with steps for access.

Now, we'll take a brief look at the course. The burn (Scottish for 'stream') which fronts the green at hole number one is similar to St

At right: **Natural look, deep bunkers and mounding: the classic style of the New Course at Grand Cypress.**

Andrews' Swilcan Burn—as is the stone bridge that crosses the burn. This is a straight-forward hole, with Scottish-style mounding much in evidence, and, of course, the stream carry to the green.

The second hole also has a stream carry off the tees and plays as a dogleg left. A monument that is set in the middle of the fairway can serve as a distance marker for tee shots, to set up a shot to the green. Additionally, two bunkers are set on the edge of a deep depression that is, in effect, the green approach. The green has three bunkers to its right.

Hole number three is a par three that features a carry across a mound and a bog to the green. The fourth hole is a dogleg left, and its knee is heavily protected with bunkers. Love-grass mounds are much in evidence here, and the green is deep and undulating.

Hole number five plays into a prevailing wind, and requires accuracy on the tee shot, which is likely to land in the vicinity of a network of pot bunkers on either side of the fairway. The green has an undulating surface. The bunkering on the right side of the fairway here is similar to 'The Principal's Nose' and 'Deacon Sime' at St Andrews.

Hole number six offers a chance to take the high road or the low road, as in the well-known Scottish ballad, with its split-level fairway, with the right side being the higher (but more level) tier. The right offers easier access to the green at the cost of slight extra yardage. The left, on the other hand, is the 'low road,' and, although seemingly the straighter, shorter route, is actually quite uneven, and is rife with pot bunkers.

The seventh hole is a par three that plays slightly uphill to a rolling green that is guarded by pot bunkers on either side. If the pin is placed to the right, a large 'catchment,' or swale, will then also figure in play.

Hole number eight is replete with beautiful vistas that could serve as distractions for the unwary. To the left of the tees is a lake, and the back tee plays out of a rough composed of lovegrass mounds. The hole plays as a dogleg right, and tee shots should be down the left center, a tactic that is dictated by the pot bunkers that are strategically located on the fairway. The green has a burn running directly in front of it, necessitating a water carry.

The ninth hole features a burn that fronts the tees, and a fairway that is cut in half by an impressive-looking belt of bunkers. Your lie would best be between these bunkers and those that pepper the green approach.

A large bunker on the left leading fairway edge of hole ten makes the obvious shot to that edge of this irregularly-shaped fairway challenging. Those golfers wanting to get in close for the stream carry to the green will find an army of bunkers surrounding the green approach.

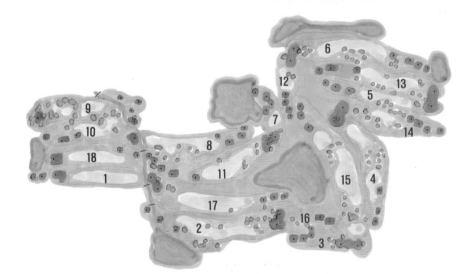

Hole	1	2	3	4	5	6	7	8	9	Out	
Blue	362	514	179	440	393	496	182	440	382	3388	
White	347	456	147	406	368	465	164	425	322	3100	
Red	332	383	116	329	304	427	132	340	309	2672	
Par	4	5	3	4	4	5	3	4	4	36	
Hole	10	11	12	13	14	15	16	17	18	In	Total
Blue	330	430	207	431	371	570	190	485	371	3385	6673
White	275	387	189	389	323	544	171	453	350	3081	6181
Red	252	301	158	296	291	491	136	410	307	2642	5314
Par	4	4	3	4	4	5	3	5	4	36	72

The wind—in conjunction with the presence of a large mound of lovegrass at the landing spot on the fairway—will determine your tee shot at hole eleven. Also, play to the right of the mound involves additional yardage, but the approach is from a better vantage point than from the shorter left side. Bunkers and a steep undulation figure in the green approach—and at left rear of the green (which slopes from right to left) is the collection swale we encountered at hole number seven.

Hole twelve is a par three, and features a long carry over two bunkers to a challenging putting green with a bunker on its left edge.

At left: **A view of the eighteenth hole at the New Course at Grand Cypress.** *Below:* **A view across a bunker of the seventh green at the New Course.**

The thirteenth is nearly a twin to the fifth hole, but is some 40 yards longer. The fairway lies between two extensive collections of pot bunkers.

The fourteenth hole plays down a hallway of bunkers to a broad, but shallow, green. Hole number fifteen is the longest on the New Course, at 570 yards. Stronger hitters may want to exercise their abilities and chance carrying over the pot bunkers, which lie 235 yards from the tees. Other players will want to lay up on the left-lying lower tier of the two-tiered fairway. A large bunker cuts across three-quarters of the fairway, and a knoll fronts the green.

Hole number sixteen is a par three with a pot bunker at front right—and a small hollow

at front left—of the green. The seventeenth hole has many features that call to mind the famous 'Road Hole' at St Andrews. Large mounds on the right side of the fairway evoke the 'sheds' or 'hotel' that golfers have to surmount to get their tee shots onto the fairway at St Andrews. On the New Course's hole seventeen, tee shots require a carry over the left edge of the mounds, and the green approach is guarded by two bunkers on the right. The green has a deep pot bunker on its right rear, and has a road and a stone wall at its left rear.

The eighteenth hole is a driving hole that has a water carry off the tees, and the green has a large hollow on its left front. This hollow is reminiscent of the 'Valley of Sin' at St Andrews, so beware.

The Bear at Grand Traverse Resort Village

Grand Traverse Village, MI USA

Grand Traverse Resort is a sports resort, conference center and real estate development on the shores of East Grand Traverse Bay in the northern part of Michigan's 'lower peninsula.' This Jack Nicklaus resort was officially opened in 1980.

The Grand Traverse area is rapidly gaining recognition as a travel destination, attracting more than five million visitors per year. The historical resonance of this area extends down through the years—from the days of the French fur trappers and their tradings with the Indians of the area to the growth of the lumber industry, to its current status as the world's largest producer of both sweet and tart cherries.

This is an area that also boasts a number of award-winning wineries, year-round recreational activities and, in the Bear at Grand Traverse Resort Village, a world-class tournament golf course designed by Jack Nicklaus. The resort spans 920 acres, including a Lake Michigan beach club. It is six miles northeast of Traverse City, Michigan, and is within a day's drive of most major midwestern cities. More than 750 spacious hotel rooms, luxurious suites and condominium villas are located on site, and a 15-story glass-enclosed tower adjoins the hotel. This tower contains, as well as luxury suites, 12,000 feet of versatile meeting and exhibit space. Meeting space in the hotel can accommodate groups of 10 to 1100; all meeting rooms are accessible from a central assembly area and include an executive board room, five 'conference hospitality parlors' and a grand ballroom that can be divided up into eight meeting rooms.

Above: **The 'Golden Bear' himself—the designer of The Bear at Grand Traverse Village.** *Below, left to right:* **A lady golfer lines up a putt on the second green; hole nine as seen from the tees; and a chip shot, out of a bunker at the thirteenth green.**

The condominiums offer studio, one bedroom, two bedroom and three bedroom accommodations that are located along the fairways of the magnificent Jack Nicklaus-designed 'The Bear' tournament course, and the Grand Traverse Resort Course, designed by Bill Newcomb, that offers a fine round of golf in its own right. Other amenities include the Traverse Pavilion, a permanent, covered, 8000 square foot patio that is available in spring, summer and fall for activities including receptions, cocktail parties, barbecues, dinners, concerts and special events, and in the winter is an ice rink.

In addition, the Beach Club on the shores of East Grand Traverse Bay is a perfect setting for an outdoor gathering, with its 4500 square foot deck, plus roaster, grill and bar service. Exhibition space is provided by the Indoor Sports Complex, featuring five tennis courts in two halls—one of 12,000 square feet, and one of 18,000 square feet—and these can be used for staging exhibitions of all sorts. The 30 foot ceilings in both halls provide more than adequate vertical clearance for all exhibition purposes.

The Grand Traverse Resort contains more than 340 contemporary-styled condominiums in a variety of resort settings, including the shores of East Grand Traverse Bay; amid the fairways of The Bear; and amid the fairways of the Grand Traverse Resort Course.

Our interest here is, naturally, focused on The Bear at Grand Traverse Village, Jack Nicklaus' great tournament course that opened in June of 1985. The Bear is a variegated, Scottish-influenced course having landscapes that come straight out of Scotland, as well as tall stands of timber that are typical of Michigan.

The Bear hosts the Michigan Bell Showdown Skins games, a popular yearly attraction. In addition, 1988 saw the introduction of the John Jacobs Practical Golf Schools, which offer both week-long and weekend sessions, and provide for meals, accommodations and carts. The Jacobs schools offer practical instruction that does not attempt to re-make the golfer, but rather teaches the individual how to make the ball behave better.

The land's natural topography makes for

holes of great beauty and unique challenge, as in the tee shot over wetlands to be found at hole number three, or the stately hardwood trees that provide a framing for the water carry at the twelfth green. Mounding and moguls add character and a quality to this stunning layout. Yardage varies considerably from front to back tees, making for an exciting test of golf for players at all levels. The Bear offers Scottish-style terraced fairways and tiered greens nestled among hardwood forests, lakes, streams and fruit orchards.

Jack Nicklaus is quoted in the Grand Traverse Resort Village brochure as saying, 'With rolling land, trees, lakes, streams and flatland, you have a mixture of different features that people will see in different places but rarely on one golf course. That's what makes this course unique. No two holes are similar.

'... As you look at most holes, you see interesting shadowing—done with the liberal use of mounding, some ledging of the fairways and grass-sided bunkers. It's a different effect.

'Greens are a little larger than normal, with a few more features to hide the pins, but still with ways for the average golfer to get in. Greens have a nice movement to them.

'... This course will not take 20 years to mature. It's almost there now.'

The first hole requires a water carry off the tees, and overflights will find the massive bunker on the left side of the fairway. Large

Above: **A view of the twelfth green and the lake that necessitates a carry there.** *Below right:* **The eighth green.** *At bottom, right:* **A view of the third hole.**

bunkers guard the right and left sides of the triangular green, and trees form a stand behind it.

Hole number two features a fairway/bunker situation similar to the first hole, and this time, the right edge of the fairway forms a drop in the direction of the green, which is framed by five bunkers.

The tree-lined third hole plays as a dogleg right, and has a row of bunkers on its left edge, where they will swallow overflights from the tees. The back tees have trees as an obstruction to their left, making the fairway shot a matter of targeting between these and the tree that stands to the fairway's right. The green approach is a stream carry, and the green slopes to the right.

Hole four is a tree-lined par three with a pond carry off the tees. The green slopes back to front, toward the pond. Hole five tees off to a fairway that is split by a stream. The more valiant will probably go for the stream carry from the tees, but should be wary of the bunker that lies on the right side of the far fairway—just in line with ball flights from the tees. The green approach is a pond carry, with a green that has a grass bunker on its left, and slopes toward the water.

Hole number six is a driver's long dogleg left. The end of the fairway and the green are framed with trees. Trees and mounds also

await overflights from the tees. The seventh features a water carry off the tees to a fairway that has bunkers guarding its right-hand side. The left edge of this fairway has a 10-foot drop. The green approach is a small valley, and grass bunkers line the left edge of the green, in concert with two sand bunkers—at left and left rear of the green.

The eighth is a dogleg right, with a lake impinging on the green approach from the right. The green has a bunker on its right side, and a bunker and heavy mounding behind it. The ninth hole is a par three that plays across the arm of a lake to a green that features a drop to the lake on its front, and slopes to the left, with bunkers right and left.

Hole number ten plays down a wide hallway of trees to a fairway with bunkers set in on its left side, where overflights from the tees are

likely to find them. Mounds flank the fairway and there is a drop off the right-hand side. A stream cuts across the fairway toward its end, and bunkers and mounds line the left side of the green approach. The green is surrounded with bunkers.

Golfers at the eleventh hole tee off amidst heavy mounding, and the fairway is accompanied on its right side by a stream that suddenly cuts across at the halfway point. Across the stream, mounds line the left side of the fairway, and a grass bunker at left and a sand bunker at right guard the green. A three-foot drop to the right of the green approach completes this scenario.

Hole number twelve requires tee shots that pass down a hallway composed of mounds on the left and trees on the right. The green approach is a lake carry to a green that slopes

toward the lake. The green has bunkers at front and rear on the right side, and at left rear. Trees also line the latter half of this hole.

The tree-lined thirteenth hole is a par three that features a lake carry to a heavily contoured green that has three massive bunkers 'out front,' and two smaller bunkers—and a pair of mounds—in back.

Hole fourteen is a dogleg left with bunkers guarding either side of the fairway at the most likely landing spot for shots from the tees. Mounding further down on the right side adds further interest here. The green slopes in toward its own center, and has mounds all around and a bunker on its exposed left front face.

The landing spot on the fifteenth has a drop to the right, and a rock bed a little farther out at the same spot. The green approach has a lake impinging from the right, and bunkers on the left—it's a treacherous passage to a triangular green having bunkers set into its sides, grass bunkers at left and right, mounds behind and the lake in front.

Hole sixteen is lined with mounds, and has a rock bed off to the right of the head of the fairway. It's a dogleg left, with a bunker sunk into the exposed left front of the green, and a bunker behind. The green slopes treacherously.

Hole seventeen is a par three that makes you tee off over a field full of mounds to a green having heavy bunkering in front of it, and bunkering to the right. The eighteenth hole features a tee shot to a two-pronged fairway, the right prong of which will save some distance to the green, but requires a tee shot over a field of mounds and past a tree to the right. The green approach is a water carry, with a treacherously sloping green. Overflights will find the grass bunkers behind the green, or the sand bunker at right rear.

Says Jack Nicklaus, in the Grand Traverse Resort Village brochure, 'I'm certain it will become one of the premier courses in the world.'

Below right, this page: **A view of the tees, the lake and some of the bunkering at the thirteenth hole.** *Above opposite:* **A sun-gilded image of one of the big bunkers that guard the first green.** *Below opposite:* **The seventeenth hole, seen from the tees. A field of mounds, and heavy bunkering, figure in this carry.**

Hole	1	2	3	4	5	6	7	8	9	Out	
Blue	393	451	528	194	413	532	423	386	168	3488	
White	352	399	472	143	376	471	364	351	142	3070	
Red	301	346	425	98	336	435	328	271	117	2657	
Par	4	4	5	3	4	5	4	4	3	36	
Hole	10	11	12	13	14	15	16	17	18	In	Total
Blue	505	421	413	167	390	543	451	220	467	3577	7065
White	446	364	361	141	347	494	379	188	386	3106	6176
Red	375	304	301	93	291	427	324	155	354	2624	5281
Par	5	1	1	3	4	5	1	3	4	36	72

These pages: **The Bear at Grand Traverse thirteenth hole. Three bunkers in front, two behind, mounds, trees and a lake are all features of this short, but tough, par three.**

Harbour Town Golf Links

Hilton Head Island, South Carolina USA

Harbour Town Golf Links, home of the MCI Heritage Classic and the PGA Seniors International, is the only golf club in the world to host both a PGA Tour event and a PGA Senior Tour event. Jack Nicklaus worked in cooperation with renowned golf course architect Pete Dye in the design of this famous course way back in 1969—when Jack, then already one of the world's renowned golfers, was just getting his start in the golf course architecture business.

The rich Scottish heritage of this course is exemplified by the use of cross-ties around the bunkers, and Centipede and Bahia grass in the roughs. This combination of grasses, kept long in height and cut, is rarely found on a US course of any kind. The earth bunkers at holes two, six and sixteen; and the pot bunkers at nine, ten and fourteen lend further Scottish flavor to this great course, which is in the upper third of *Golf* magazine's '100 Greatest Courses in the World' listing. This great course is also among the top six courses of *USA Today*'s '130 Best-Designed Courses in the USA.'

Harbour Town Golf Links is one of three golf layouts at the fabulous Sea Pines Resort on Hilton Head Island, with the other two being the Ocean and Sea Marsh courses, which also offer a fine test of golf, and were designed by George Cobb.

Now, let's take a tour. The back tees at hole one face a water carry, and the ball must be kept low to avoid the overhanging branches of the trees that line this hole. The green is protected by one large sand bunker out front, and two grass bunkers behind.

Hole number two has an earth bunker off to the left of the landing area, ready for over-flights. Glimpses of ponds hidden among the trees on either side could serve as a distraction here, and the earth bunker to the right of the green approach could catch the errant green-ward shot. The green is set obliquely to the fairway. The green approach is pinched by trees on either side, and other greenery complicates matters here. A grass bunker and two sand bunkers guard the sides of the green, and more trees stand sentinel behind. A challenging par five.

The third hole is a hallway of trees, with a large bunker on the left front of the green, and four smaller bunkers and water on the right.

It's a small green, and rather hard to stay on. Hole four is a par three with a lot of water off the tees and a large, hidden bunker—and more water—behind the green. Beware of hooks and overflights here.

The fifth is a dogleg right with bunkers lining it at strategic points, and some dangerous water to the left. The green is hard to hit, and has two all-too-easy-to-find bunkers to its left. On its right are overhanging trees,

and behind it is greenery that could snag your ball. The green falls off to the right and to the rear.

Hole six is a dogleg right, with a pond and an earth bunker on the right. These work in counterpoise to the trees, rooted in the fairway on the left. It's either lay up, or play long and accurate off the tees here. The green has two bunkers left, one bunker right and pampas grass at left, right, and rear.

The seventh hole is a tough little par three that features a carry over water and a massive bunker to the green. The green is narrow but deep, and sand surrounds it on all sides but right rear, where trees stand guard. Trees also guard the green at left front and left rear, with a hiatus between that is filled by yet more sand. You'll earn this one.

Below: **Golfers at the first green of Harbour Town Golf Links. Note the cross-ties around the bunker.**

Hole number ten is a dogleg left with a pond on its left, and an approach that is tree-choked. The green is nestled in the trees with a pair of bunkers to its right. The rearmost of these sports a nasty bit of greenery in its middle, making double trouble for errant balls in that quarter.

The eleventh hole is another hallway of trees, with water on either side as well. The green is protected by a tree at right front, and bunkering at left and right along its sides. This is a verdant challenge, indeed.

The twelfth hole is a dogleg right with trees guarding either side of the fairway. This calls for a long tee shot to reach the dogleg, and then it's a shot to a radically-shaped green that is heavily bunkered on its forward half. The shape of the green could make a big difference in the way it is played, depending upon pin placement.

A bunker on the left side of the thirteenth hole's fairway awaits tee shots there; and a bunker farther down—on the right side of the fairway—complicates the green approach, which features trees on either side, and a massive bunker fronting the green. Behind the green, a grass bunker awaits overflights. This is a par four that will be earned by anyone escaping without extra strokes.

Trees and grass bunkers guard the left side, while a lake guards the front and right, of the green at hole number fourteen, a par three with a small, round green that is a difficult target indeed. The pot bunker at left rear will catch overpowered tee shots, and pampas grass awaits the unlucky overflights to right rear. There's lots of water on this one.

The fifteenth hole has trees all along the right, and trees on the left, with the accompaniment of a lake along the left of the green approach. Thoughtful shot making is demanded here, as a bunker lies right, opposite the water. The very small green has bunkers left and right that form pincers at its front. A natural bunker lies at left rear, and trees guard the right rear.

Hole eight is a dogleg left with trees and ponds guarding the fairway. Two trees about two-thirds of the way down form a 'gunsight' that must be negotiated, and the wayward green shot may find the water to the right and left there, or the long strip bunker on the green's left. Overflights will find the bunker behind the green, which is ominously decorated with ball-snagging pampas grass.

The ninth hole has a tight border of trees on its last 100 yards, and the vee shaped green is superimposed upon a wedge-shaped bunker that points at a companion bunker behind the green. This shallow green will be hard to hold, so accuracy and good judgement are paramount here.

Above left: **Water, sand, and a challenging surface: the seventeenth green.** *At right:* **The eighteenth green, with Harbour Town Lighthouse and picturesque Calibogue Sound for a backdrop.**

Hole	1	2	3	4	5	6	7	8	9	Out	
Heritage	397	492	399	188	528	404	165	439	327	3339	
Men's	326	474	314	146	510	363	124	385	310	2952	
Ladies'	300	413	297	125	407	302	63	341	249	2527	
Par	4	5	4	3	5	4	3	4	4	36	
Hole	10	11	12	13	14	15	16	17	18	In	Total
Heritage	418	412	404	363	153	561	373	169	458	3311	6650
Men's	350	371	379	320	121	472	294	137	428	2872	5824
Ladies'	323	312	290	300	88	407	250	85	330	2385	4912
Par	4	4	4	4	3	5	4	3	4	35	71

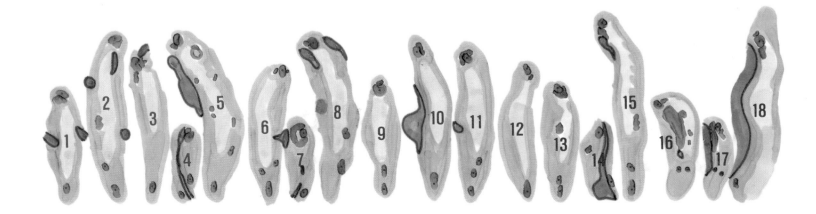

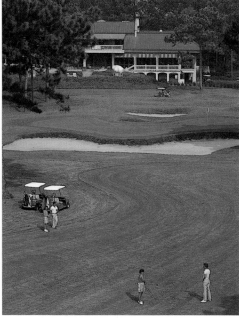

Above: A golfer faces the first green approach. *Below, at bottom:* A foursome on the seventeenth hole. *At left:* Playing out of a bunker on the thirteenth. *Overleaf:* An aerial view of the seventh green.

Hole number sixteen is a dogleg left with trees squeezing in from the right and a massive earth bunker all along the left. In addition, a pond just to the left of the inner tees causes some distraction, and a bad hook could find its way there. The green is surrounded by bunkers and will prove to be a slippery target.

The seventeenth hole is a par three that demands a bold and extremely accurate shot to a narrow, irregular green that has a 90 yard bunker at its exposed face, and lots of water between it and the tees. A bunker behind the green will catch any overflights to the inland side. A crosswind can easily blow shots into the lagoon at left.

The eighteenth hole is thought of as the 'gem' of Harbour Town Golf Links. A long carry off the tee will reach the bulge of fairway that juts to the left, into Calibogue Sound. The right is guarded by greenery, and less valorous players may try to avoid the water carry by playing to the right—it's a slender margin, and you'll have a terrible time with the flora. A long, golf-tee shaped bunker holds the green in its 'cup,' and a pot bunker is at the rear of the green. Calibogue Sound is on the immediate left, and there's mounding to the right. This par four is an outstanding finish to a great 18 holes of golf.

The Hills of Lakeway Golf Club

Austin, Texas USA

Above and at right: **The seventh hole waterfall at the Hills of Lakeway. It's a challenging par three hole, and the water's distracting beauty adds to the challenge.**

The Hills of Lakeway is a new residential and sports club development located 20 miles northwest of Austin in the Hill Country, as it is called, around Lake Travis. The resort is a private one, with residential units weaving in and our among the fairways of the development's three 18-hole golf courses, two of which—Yaupon and Live Oak—have excellent local reputations, and one of which—The Hills course—was designed by Jack Nicklaus, and is legendary.

The Hills course was voted 'Favorite Golf Course' in a poll of golf professionals of southern Texas and Louisiana that was conducted by *Gulf Coast Golfer* magazine, the results of which were listed in that magazine's January/February 1987 issue. This magnificent course was also cited as one of the best in the state of Texas in *Golf Digest*'s November 1985 article 'The Best in Each State.'

The seventh hole at the Hills of Lakeway is rapidly becoming one of the most famous—and most photographed—holes in the US. It is a spectacular par three with a 15-foot waterfall in front of the green. Mr Nicklaus began designing the course in 1979, and it was opened for play in 1981. Water comes into play on 11 of the 18 holes, and a huge double green, reminiscent of St Andrews in Scotland, serves the eighth and twelfth holes, while the eleventh has a huge bunker with grass islands.

Running through the course is limestone-bottomed Hurst Creek, a Hill Country stream with natural waterfalls. The course features a multiple-tee setup that enables golfers at any level to enjoy a challenging test of golf. The back tees are intensely difficult, and the course played at this level is one of the ultimate tests of golf.

The Hills of Lakeway is a very beautiful course, and is complete with a Nicklaus-designed three-hole practice facility that can be played from either end for a good test of one's abilities in most wind situations. The practice facility is part of the Lakeway Academy of Golf in the Hills.

The Academy of Golf in the Hills offers a unique approach to full instruction on all the facets of the game. This approach is tailored to the individual strengths of each player, and is geared to helping players develop their game to their individual best. Pros and amateurs alike have lauded this program, with its full array of technological aids and good, common sense instruction by some of golfing's finest instructors.

Mike Adams, known as the 'Swing Doctor,' teaches more than 30 tour players, and is an acknowledged authority on the vicissitudes of the golf swing; also, he's one of the best short-game instructors in the country. Mike is co-director of the academy. Bill Moretti has a national reputation as an instructor, and teaches more than 20 tour players. Clay Edwards was head professional at Victoria Country Club for five years before joining the Academy, and has developed a solid following on the PGA Tour.

Dr Jim Suttie, the 'Golf Professor,' currently teaches more than 25 tour players and advises the golf pros on how to teach others. Mike McGetrick was previously an instructor with Golf Dynamics Golf Schools. Mark Steinbauer was the director of the North Texas Academy of Golf; this bright young teacher already has one best-selling instruction video, *Golf Made Easy*, to his credit.

Students are grouped within handicap levels, and clinics are open to all levels of golfers, from the total beginner to the professional. Customized programs are available, as well as individual instruction. The Academy is open to members and non-members of the Hills of Lakeway club. There are a variety of intensive programs, for both weekends and weekdays, as well as a VIP School and Junior School, to accommodate every golfer's needs.

Of course, the whole Lakeway complex is magnificent—from its golf courses and complete tennis facilities, to its boating and other outdoor activities facilities. The focus of our interest here is the Jack Nicklaus-designed Hills of Lakeway golf course. There are restrictions as to who can play the Hills course, as this is a private development, but golfers worldwide will want to know this great course.

The following is a hole-by-hole tour of the Hills of Lakeway golf course. The first hole, a dogleg right with a stream carry from the back tee, is the longest hole on the course. Two bunkers on the green approach threaten balls that are hooked to the left, and the green is protected by a bunker on its left. A carry over rough will get you there.

Hole number two is a par three with a bunker protecting the exposed face of the green. Trees often figure in play on this course, as on the third hole, where tee shots—

especially from the back tees—must negotiate a hallway of trees. This hole is a dogleg left with a bunker placed where most tee shots will have to carry over it to get good yardage on the fairway. The obliquely-set green has a bunker on its left front face.

The fourth hole has bunkers and greenery on both sides of the fairway, where tee shots are likely to land—no hook shots here. The green is tucked to the right, behind a bunker, and trees surround it. It's a great challenge. Hole number five plays along a serpentine fairway with a bunker placed in such a manner that accuracy is demanded of tee shots. The green is well-bunkered and is set back in a grove of trees.

Hole number six plays to a contoured fairway, and its green fronts on Hurst Creek. Overflights will find the huge bunker behind the green, and hooked shots will find the bunkers to the left. This one gets you ready for the justly famous seventh hole at the Hills of Lakeway.

The par three seventh is stunning. You stand at your tee and look at the green and what you see, on the opposite side of the considerable expanse of running stream at your feet, is the glistening cascade of a 15-foot high waterfall in front of the green. The scenic beauty alone is enough to distract, and the intimidation of facing this, with its torrents cascading past your line of sight, is consider-

able. Take heart, your strength will not fail—in fact, bunkers back the green to catch over-powered balls. This is one par you'll earn.

The eighth hole has a water carry off the tees, plays down a straightforward fairway, and has a water carry on the green approach. Though this hole lets you loosen up a bit after the rigors of the seventh, it presents its own kind of challenge. The dogleg left ninth hole has a 'gunsight' composed of two trees on the fairway, just about where you'll be thinking of making the green approach, with a bunker to carry over to the triangular green.

Hole number ten is a long dogleg left, with a bunker to the left of the landing spot and a well-protected green. The eleventh is a

Hole	1	2	3	4	5	6	7	8	9	Out	
Gold	537	197	463	418	424	402	165	405	495	3506	
Blue	496	159	425	400	399	376	151	378	480	3264	
White	468	135	381	368	383	313	134	358	453	2993	
Red	400	116	352	340	334	293	95	275	429	2634	
Par	5	3	4	4	4	4	3	4	5	36	
Hole	10	11	12	13	14	15	16	17	18	In	Total
Gold	424	518	185	356	178	368	375	505	418	3327	6833
Blue	403	498	146	311	156	310	365	481	397	3067	6331
White	374	475	138	294	133	310	330	451	372	2877	5870
Red	303	449	119	268	117	247	307	403	276	2489	5123
Par	4	5	3	4	3	4	4	5	4	36	72

At left: **Lofting a tee shot over the seventh hole water-fall to the green. Note the handsome, rustic rockwork that frames the waterfall, which is part of Hurst Creek.** *Above right:* **A golfer prepares to tee off amidst the scenic beauty of the Hill Country—northwest of Austin, Texas—at the Hills of Lakeway.**

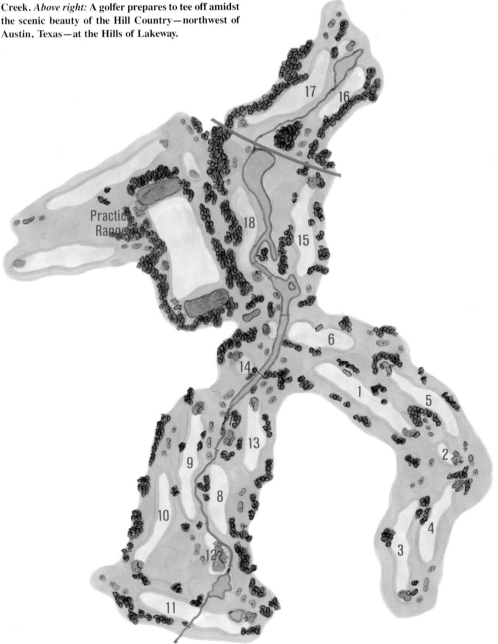

delayed dogleg left that features a carry over two branches of Hurst Creek to a green that hides behind an enormous bunker with grass islands. Hole number twelve, a par three, shares its green with hole eight. A stream carry off the tees gets you to the rather slippery green. Good luck.

Golfers at hole thirteen tee off to a tree-lined fairway, and thence the play is toward a green that is practically smothered with bunkers. The fourteenth hole is another par three, with a carry across Hurst Creek to a well-bunkered green. Again, it's water and sand, and a not-so-easy par.

Hole number fifteen features a carry across one of the widest parts of Hurst Creek from the back tees, while the next level tees off from a peninsula somewhat closer—but still a water carry—to the fairway, while the innermost tees avoid the water, which is then off to the left of the fairway. The green has a crescent-shaped bunker on its left side, cutting around to protect the approach. An exciting hole.

The sixteenth hole is a dogleg left, with its green approach a carry across Hurst Creek to a green with trees behind it. Hole number seventeen is a tree-lined dogleg right which demands accuracy all the way. The green approach features multiple bunkers on the left up to the left side of the green itself, and the rightward setting of the green will feed many wind-blown shots to the bunkers.

The back tees at the eighteenth hole have a very long water carry—lengthwise over a bend in Hurst Creek—and the inner tees also have to carry over the stream, which flows along the left side of the fairway, and necessitates another stream carry at the green approach. The green has the stream all along its left and left rear. It's a great finish to a sensational 18 holes of unique, championship golf at the Hills of Lakeway.

La Paloma Country Club

Tucson, Arizona USA

La Paloma means 'The Dove.' This development is a 790-acre, master-planned community luxury resort, golf course and country club. It features a Jack Nicklaus-designed golf course, 1600 prime residential properties, plus the Westin La Paloma—a 488-room world-class luxury resort and convention facility. The residential units are planned around the centerpiece of the 27-hole Nicklaus-designed course.

The course is a target golf course that was designed for desert conditions—requiring approximately one-half the amount of grass as most temperate-climate courses—and uses low-water consumption native plants to frame the fairways. Mr Nicklaus personally supervised the construction of the course, adjusting his plans where needed to ensure a minimum of disturbance to the natural flora.

A lot of planning and painstaking care was required to create this natural desert course, which has not even one water hazard. The course was designed with the preservation of wildlife habitats and the encouragement of the proliferation of native animals in mind.

La Paloma's three nines are the Hill, Ridge and Canyon courses—names which describe the distinctive landscape of each location. There are multiple tee settings for each hole, and each green has multiple pin placements, which means golfers of all levels will find their challenge at La Paloma. With the aforementioned variables in mind, plus that fact that golfers can combine nines into a large number of 18-hole rounds of golf, the variety of challenge, and the *character* of that challenge, is far more than enough for any golfer's grandest dreams.

Let's take a tour of this fine desert golf course, taking the Hill Nine as our opening layout, and going on 'in' on the Canyon Nine, and then considering a 'rise to the heights' on the Ridge Nine as a possible alternate finishing setup.

Hole one of the Hill Nine at La Paloma plays uphill, with distraction provided by the splendor of the Santa Catalina Mountains, which fill the background. A small bunker on the left may catch some tee shots, and a large bunker along the right guards the approach to a softly contoured green.

The second hole has a massive bunker all along the right side of the fairway, and the

Above and above left: **Views of La Paloma, a natural desert course.** *Above opposite:* **The saguaro-shadowed fairway bunker and the green of the Hill ninth.** *Below opposite:* **A view down the length of Canyon four.**

green approach has a necklace of pot bunkers that front a small valley. The elevated green is nestled among grass mounds, and has bunkers in front and behind. The tee shot at hole number three must reach a high plateau, and then it's a drive along a dogleg right fairway to a green that is sandwiched between two bunkers. Some greenery intrudes toward the green approach from the left. This is the longest hole on any of the three La Paloma nines, at 561 yards. A driver's challenge.

Golfers at par three hole number four tee off over a natural wash to a tri-level green that is protected by a long, diagonal bunker on its front left, plus a grass swale and small mounds. Hole number five is a dogleg right with a fairway that is forked at the green approach. This necessitates accuracy, as a rough divides the two 'prongs,' the rightmost of which is nearest the green. Stroke-shaving shots to the green will necessitate a carry over a bunker and grass hollows on its right. On the left is a grass swale.

The sixth hole plays downhill into a landing place with a bunker just ahead, to the right. The green approach on this plant-rimmed par

four is a desert swale. Hole number seven requires shots from all but the forward tee to carry over a plant-choked wash to the fairway. The wash is ever present on the right, and cuts across the green approach to become a threat on the left of the green. A bunker rides the right face of this small green. A real desert challenge.

Another par three, hole number eight has a carry over a low, overgrown valley from the tees to the contoured green. The green is guarded on three sides by bunkers and grassy mounds. Hole nine's every indication is to aim your long tee shot to the right of the fairway in order to make this demanding par four shorter; accuracy is needed here, though—a huge bunker follows the fairway all along the right. The green approach is over a deep valley to a small green that is guarded by grass mounds.

Now we'll tour La Paloma's Canyon Nine. Golfers at the Canyon Nine's first hole tee off across desert terrain to a large landing area that is guarded by a pot bunker on the left. The green is guarded by a deep, trifoil bunker at right front, and a barbell-shaped bunker at right rear. This green is incorporated into an existing landform to create a natural amphitheater for your shot to the pin.

Hole two on the Canyon Nine is a downhill, sharp dogleg right with a deep canyon all along its right side. The tri-lobed green is 40 feet lower than the tees, and has a bunker set into each of its interior curves. It's a very challenging introduction to this nine, and is aesthetically stunning in the bargain. The third hole is a par three that features a carry over a large canyon to a split-level hillside green that is guarded on either side by strategically placed bunkers and a giant saguaro cactus.

Canyon hole number four features a high hillside tee shot onto a tapering, serpentine fairway that lies in a deep valley. A natural wash guards the right side of the fairway and the green is additionally guarded by grass hollows—and a large bunker on its right front.

The fifth hole is a long dogleg left, with grass mounds all around the landing spot. The green approach is a natural wash, and the green has a large bunker at left front, and a smaller bunker at right rear. Golfers teeing off

at hole number six will have to carry over a gently sloping desert terrain to a wide fairway. Bunkers off to the left will entrap overflights from the tees, and the terraced green is cut into a hillside. A massive bunker guards the front of the green. It's a very enjoyable challenge.

Canyon hole number seven is loaded with scenic distraction, but you should do your best to keep your attention focused. The fairway has a large wash to its left, and a sloping hill on its right. The wash cuts across the green approach, and the green is contoured and sharply cut into a hillside. A bunker guards the front. Be on your game here.

The eighth hole is the longest par three on the course, at 211 yards from the back tees. Tee shots here must pass over natural vegetation to a green having a large bunker with grass islands on its left. This bunker also figures in tee shots from the back tees.

The ninth hole on the La Paloma Canyon Nine is a long dogleg right, with two dangerous bunkers to the left of the landing spot, and a long grass bunker to the right. An eight-foot deep grass bunker guards the green approach. It's a great ending for this round of golf.

After that test of golfing skill, let's posit the Ridge Nine as alternate ending for the Hill Nine. In other words, we've just conquered the valley—so now let's swoop into the heights.

The first hole of the Canyon Nine faces the Santa Catalinas, as did hole number one on the Hill Nine—as if to remind you that 'the mountain' is still to be surmounted. This is a different, but not less splendid, view of the mountains—a factor that threatens to distract you as you stand on your elevated tee position. You're going to have to carry across the desert to a fairway that is guarded on the left with a line of bunkers. Don't hook here. The narrow green has bunkers on either side.

The Ridge Nine's second hole also has elevated tees. Shots to the fairway carry over native vegetation, and there is the danger of going too long or too far left, where the outer curve of the fairway will leave you in the rough. A large, long bunker guards the approach to the contoured, hillside green, which is additionally protected by grassy hollows.

The third hole is a dogleg right that could, even more easily than the previous hole, leave you in the rough at left, or in the bunker at right. The green approach is a carry over deep grass mounds, hollows and bunkers. The green has bunkers at left and right.

The fourth hole on the Ridge Nine is said to be the most picturesque par three at La Paloma. You tee off across the lip of a 40-foot canyon to a green that is protected by bunkers that could easily draw errant shots in. Accuracy is the key, and the green provides further

Above: **The third green of the Canyon Nine: bunkers, canyon and cactus. La Paloma has not even one water hazard.** *At right:* **A brilliantly designed hole.**

challenge—rolls and depressions divide it into three distinctly different pin placement areas.

Hole number five has bunkering the entire length of the fairway on the left, and scenic greenery that fronts a 60-foot canyon on the right. It's a dogleg left, with bunkering on the left of the green approach. The sixth hole is a long dogleg left, with a single, massive longi-

tudinal bunker from just below its 'knee' to the end of the green on the right side. Overflights will find the huge bunker, and hollows, as well as a lobe of the aforementioned bunker, guard the green approach.

A par three, the seventh hole plays across a valley and a sand trap to a small hillside green. The inner tees avoid the sand trap. Hole number eight is a sharp dogleg left that is guarded all along its inner bend by a massive longitudinal bunker similar to that we encountered at holes number five and six. This hole necessitates a carry over desert from the back tees. At its 'knee,' opposite the giant bunker, is a smaller bunker that is set cannily to catch hooks and overflights to the right. The multi-level green has a large bunker guarding its front and left side, and a smaller bunker in its concave back.

The ninth hole on the Ridge Nine is the second longest on the La Paloma nines, at 560 yards. The back tees must carry a beautiful natural valley to a fairway that is a driving delight. The green is surrounded by deep grass mounds and hollows, and has a bunker directly in front. This is an exuberant hole, and a great way to cap off the intricacies that have gone before, or from which to proceed on—to the intriguing challenge of either the Hill, or the Canyon, Nine.

Hill

Hole	1	2	3	4	5	6	7	8	9	Total	
Gold	340	381	561	185	467	419	538	157	415	3463	
Blue	320	321	484	171	421	385·	516	132	391	3141	
White	282	306	476	162	409	340	491	124	374	2964	
Red	225	271	383	94	348	302	421	84	302	2430	
Par	4	4	5/4	3	4	4	5	3	4	36/35	

Canyon

Hole	1	2	3	4	5	6	7	8	9	Total	
Gold	454	514	178	417	542	355	445	211	418	3534	
Blue	417	497	166	383	517	337	426	190	379	3312	
White	384	434	158	314	510	268	407	160	356	2991	
Red	356	363	113	289	445	228	368	134	331	2627	
Par	4	5/4	3	4	5	4	4	3	4	36/35	

Ridge

Hole	1	2	3	4	5	6	7	8	9	Total	
Gold	381	411	517	199	420	459	171	436	560	3554	
Blue	364	374	482	176	381	449	153	395	549	3323	
White	314	334	470	158	349	431	132	369	463	3020	
Red	264	309	372	112	306	262	105	285	433	2448	
Par	4	4	5/4	3	4	4	3	4	5	35/36	

The Loxahatchee Club

Jupiter, Florida USA

The Loxahatchee Club is a master-planned community with a Jack Nicklaus-designed members' golf course as its centerpiece. Also included in the project are four tennis courts, full swimming facilities and excellent dining amenities.

Loxahatchee was developed by Canadians Gordon Gray and Brian Magee, and is limited to 325 memberships, which are available only to property owners in the residential community of the surrounding complex.

The golf course was named the 'Best New Private Course of the Year' by *Golf Digest* magazine in 1985. The criteria used in making this assessment were shot values, playability, design balance, memorability and aesthetics. Jack Nicklaus, as quoted in a Loxahatchee publicity release, states, 'One should take into consideration that Loxahatchee was not planned as a tournament course. It is a course for members.' The West German magazine *Golf/Tennis/Polo* stated in their January 1987 issue that 'Whoever knows the course counts it among the best and most beautiful in the USA.'

Loxahatchee got its name from a Seminole Indian word that means 'Turtle River.' Loxahatchee is built on land that was a flat, desolate 750-acre dairy farm. That land has obviously been transformed, in part by the relocation of some one million square feet of earth that was excavated in the formation of Loxahatchee's 85 acres of lakes.

This is a very Scottish-influenced course, with mounds and moguls covered with flowering lovegrass that frame target areas, a double green serving holes thirteen and fifteen, and an island green at the sixteenth hole. Each of the holes has its own distinctions, with Scottish style fairways, native trees and other Florida vegetation imparting a special kind of scenic beauty.

It is said that the level of difficulty at this course changes with the weather. When the weather is cooperative, the course is a good test of golf. When the high winds that sometimes come to visit Loxahatchee are in action, the course is tougher by far. But, whatever your personal level of play, Loxahatchee can meet you with a challenge appropriate to your level, thanks to its several tee placements, many of which also change the angle of play on the course.

Above: **A taste of the Scottish flavor of Loxahatchee.** *At left:* **A backward glance from the eleventh green.** *Above opposite:* **Mounds and water on the seventeenth.**

The round, bentgrass greens are a rarity in tropical climates like that of Florida, and the mounds are typically 40 feet high. There are steep-faced bunker walls, plateau fairways and deep, gaping grass bunkers. The clubhouse is elevated to overlook the ninth, tenth and eighteenth holes—and a waterfall cascades down from behind it, welcoming golfers at the eighteenth as they come 'home.'

Loxahatchee is 7043 yards from the back tees, 6064 from the foremost tees. A typical hole is the eleventh, where a tee shot directly over a huge bunker leaves a relatively simple pitch to the green, but a safer tee shot leaves a longer shot to the green.

The following is a hole-by-hole description of this fine course. The back tee at hole number one has a long lake carry to a rolling fairway that is bordered on both sides by wooded mounds. A large bunker is located on the right front of the green. Hole number two is a par three with a lake carry off the tees to a crescent green. Between the 'horns' of the green lies a crescent bunker, and from the front to the right rear is the lake.

The third hole has a lake to the right of the tees, and plays along an elevated fairway to a green approach that has a bunker on its left. The large, rolling, low-lying green has three

deep bunkers on its left, and mounds on the right. Hole number four has water all along its right. This hole is a dogleg right, and a large bunker rides the right of the green approach and the right front of the green. Beyond the bunker is the lake. The green is set amidst a stand of water oaks.

Golfers at the fifth hole have a short water carry from the back tees, and tee off to a deep and narrow rolling green that fronts on a bunker, and has a bunker on its right side, to catch overflights and hooked balls. Hole number six is a water carry from the back tees. The fairway is split by an estuary of the lake, which pools in front of the green. Some golfers will want to lay up here, while others will go for the long water carry to the wide, shallow green. It's an exciting hole.

The seventh hole plays along a serpentine fairway, with a bunker just to the right of the

Hole	1	2	3	4	5	6	7	8	9	Out	
Gold	372	180	462	541	163	395	437	501	431	3482	
Blue	315	162	431	512	137	374	414	476	405	3226	
Green	286	145	398	497	127	339	365	443	382	2982	
Red	258	130	371	436	101	275	344	404	352	2698	
Par	4	3	4	5	3	4	4	5	4	36	
Hole	**10**	**11**	**12**	**13**	**14**	**15**	**16**	**17**	**18**	**In**	**Total**
Gold	445	398	217	513	424	370	585	170	439	3561	7043
Blue	410	371	176	499	413	368	550	154	401	3342	6568
Green	380	338	162	471	384	335	502	134	376	3082	6064
Red	338	303	123	415	346	252	462	103	347	2689	5387
Par	4	4	3	5	4	4	5	3	4	36	72

landing area. The elevated green is protected by a huge bunker on its left front, and grass mounds on its periphery block your vision. It's best to take an extra moment to consider this hole. Hole number eight plays uphill, with water all along its right. Two bunkers to the left of the landing area could cause trouble, and the ever-present water on the right can swallow a lot of mis-hit balls. The view of the whole course here is magnificent.

The ninth hole is one of the more difficult on the Loxahatchee course—an elevated green and mounds on the right make this a challenge indeed. This is a great hole with which to finish your initial nine. Now we'll head 'in' on holes ten through eighteen. The tenth hole has water and a longitudinal bunker on its left side. To the right are trees, so it's straight up the middle here. Beware of hooks to the green—a massive bunker stretches from the left green approach to the cheek of the green itself.

Hole number eleven. Beware the wind and mounding here. Bunkers displace the fairway near the landing spot, and water all along the right helps to create a narrow tunnel of play-

Above right: **A view of the tenth green approach. The large bunker that guards the green approach can be glimpsed to the left.** *At right:* **A greenward view of the sixth hole, on which water hazards abound.**

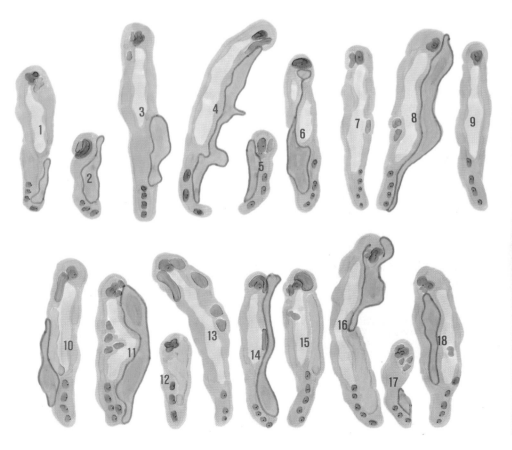

ability. The green has two bunkers at its right. These both terminate at the water. It's a very challenging hole.

Hole twelve is the longest par three on the course, and plays over a huge bunker. It is said that the long hitter has an advantage here. The thirteenth hole's tees are bordered by the largest mounds on the course. The double green is shared with hole fifteen. There are grass mounds on both sides, and a line of bunkers along the right side of the green and the green approach, and a single, huge bunker along the left.

The fourteenth hole has water on the right from tees to past the green. This is said to be the most difficult hole on the course on windy days. Hills lie to the left. The green is surrounded—by a single crescent bunker—on three sides, plus there's water to the right and right rear.

Hole number fifteen shares its green with the thirteenth hole. With a huge bunker all along the fairway's right, and strategically placed mounds, plus bunkers on the fairway, absolute accuracy is demanded here. The green is truly a 'target,' as it is canted to the

Above, at top: **A rarefied low-sun angle photo of this very beautiful course.** *Above:* **The ninth tees evince an aesthetically appealing naturalness.** *At right:* **A view down the length of the very challenging seventh.**

right, and has a huge crescent bunker on its right and rear, and a bunker 'goatee' at its chin.

At 585 yards, the sixteenth hole is the longest on the course. A large bunker borders the tees on the right and continues on up the fairway, where it abuts a lake that borders the fairway on up the right side to surround the island green. This is a driving hole, and wind from the northwest is said to increase the challenge here.

Hole number seventeen is a par three that addresses a green with deep bunkering in front, and a strategically-placed bunker at rear. The eighteenth, like the ninth hole, points you at the clubhouse. A fairway bunker will cause extra consideration at the tees. Going left will shorten the hole, but water rides this fairway all along that side. Accuracy is, again, the key. The green is canted around the edge of the pond, and has a bunker on its left, fronting the pond.

The Melrose Club

Daufuskie Island, South Carolina USA

The Melrose Club complex occupies 662 acres of land on historic Daufuskie Island—a 5000-acre barrier island on the southeastern corner of the South Carolina coast, one mile across Calibogue Sound from Hilton Head Island.

Daufuskie Island has been occupied since at least the 1600s by successive generations of Native American settlers, English settlers and Civil War-era planters. Interestingly, the island has most recently been occupied by approximately 60 descendants of former slaves who speak their own dialect—known as 'Gullah'—and who maintain age-old African customs and traditions.

Melrose is an exclusive members-only resort. In addition to its 18-hole Jack Nicklaus golf course and fully equipped golf and tennis clubhouse, it is composed of a master-planned community of 100 luxurious beach cottages, an interdenominational chapel, two miles of Atlantic beach, a fully-equipped tennis facility designed by tennis champion Stan Smith, an equestrian center, a health club, beach club, fishing lakes, crabbing docks and the 52-room, ocean-front Melrose Inn, built on the site of the legendary Melrose Mansion, which burned down in 1912.

Construction of the Melrose facilities began in 1985, and construction on the golf course was completed in September of 1986. On 4 June 1987, Jack Nicklaus shot a one-under-par 71 inaugural round of golf on the new 7052-yard course at its formal opening.

Jack Nicklaus is quoted by the Melrose publicity as saying that the course was designed to 'enhance, restore and preserve' the Daufuskie Island landscape. 'The goal was to create a course of note with a visually striking layout that rewards the smart player without making it so difficult that all the fun is gone.'

He compared the course to Shoal Creek in Birmingham, Alabama—site of the 1984 PGA Championship, and chosen to host that prestigious event again in 1990. Jack himself is a member of the Melrose Club, and maintains a residence here.

Sports Editor Terry Bunton, of *The Island Packet*, puts his feelings about Melrose this way: '… [T]he new Melrose Golf Course is quite simply a classic golf course.' This great new course was built to harmonize with its

Above: **The island of trees in the middle of the seventh fairway.** *At right:* **The beautiful and challenging lake at Melrose hole number thirteen.**

natural surroundings, not to change them. Therefore, golfers at Melrose play amid pine forests, salt and fresh water marshes and moss-draped oaks. The Atlantic Ocean is featured at the magnificent eighteenth hole.

Now, let's take a tour of this fine new course. Hole number one tees off over a tidal salt marsh to a fairway that has extensive bunkering on its left. The green here is well protected. The second hole features an oblique lake carry off the tees, with trees lining the fairway on both sides. The forward tees play straight on to the fairway.

Hole number three gives golfers more than one choice of play. In addition to its multiple tee setup, hole three has a fairway that features two routes of play at the green approach. Golfers must tee off between two trees, and then comes the decision of which we have spoken. On the left side of a tree which stands on the fairway's midpoint is a lake carry that considerably shortens the distance to the green. On the right of the tree is a dogleg left that eliminates the water danger, but will require—due to the presence of trees on the left—an extra stroke. The water carry is a precarious shot indeed, as golfers taking that route must make a precision shot between two trees, and must carry a lake and the bunker that fronts the green, which is well guarded against either approach.

Hole number four is a tree-lined dogleg right, with a carry over marshland to the green. The green has marsh on its right, and trees close in on its left. The fifth hole is, at 162 yards, the longest par three on the course. Golfers here tee off over marshland to a well-protected green.

The sixth hole has overhanging trees on either side of its fairway, and all tee shots must carry over marshland. The green has two bunkers on the right, and one bunker on the left. Golfers at hole number seven tee off over a wide expanse of marshland to a fairway that is split by an island of trees with a narrow, but deep, bunker in its center. If you go left, you'll cut the distance to the green, but there's a lot of wetland marsh on the perimeter of the fairway here, and a tree guards the green approach—which is a plateau—on the left, making the green a difficult target. Bunkers at front left and at right will come into play for all but the most accurate shots here. If you take the right approach, you'll add a stroke to your score, and the green will be a challenge, with bunkers right and left front, and marshland on the left.

The eighth hole features a carry over a stream and marshland to a tree-framed green

with marsh all along its front. Hole number nine is a 584-yard (from the back tees) double dogleg left, with a marshland carry from the tees. Trees and a bunker are set strategically on the fairway, trees are all along the right, and marshland lines the left side. The green approach features another carry over marshland to a tree-backed green having a bunker on its right front, and marshland at front and at left. It's an exuberant finish for an outstanding nine going 'out.'

Hole ten features a carry from the tees over marshland to a serpentine fairway lined with trees. The green nestles into a grove of trees, is bunkered all along its right, and has a bunker at left rear. The eleventh hole is a tree-lined dogleg right with a plateau fairway having a bunker that guards against tee shots. The green likewise has a bunker that is set in on its face in such a way that accuracy of range is a necessity here. Bunkers at rear and right rear, plus trees all around, add to the defenses here.

The twelfth is a long, straightforward hole that features a lake carry from the back tees, a 'gunsight' of trees on the fairway at the halfway point, and a monstrous bunker across the green approach. The green has a tree and the huge aforementioned bunker at right, a bunker at left front, and trees and a lake at right rear. Overflights could also wind up in the marshland at rear.

Hole number thirteen is a par three that demands a lengthy lake carry from the back tees. The green fronts on the lake and has bunkers set in on either side at rear. Trees, rough and marshland further emphasize the need for concentration here.

Golfers on holes fourteen and fifteen will see the gleam of a lake through the trees, about halfway down either fairway. The fourteenth is a tree-lined dogleg right, with a carry over rough from the tees to a fairway that has overhanging trees on either side at its midpoint. The green has bunkers at right and left front, and has a grassy swale all along its rear and left side.

The fifteenth is a reverse of the previous hole. Here, you tee off beside the swale and play along the fairway between overhanging trees, but have the added presence of a treacherous, long bunker, partially hidden by the trees, down the fairway's right side to and including the green approach. The approach is a carry over rough to a green having a bunker at right rear, and trees everywhere but in front.

The back tee at par three hole number sixteen has to carry over a lot of sand to a green that nestles into the trees and has hollows on both sides, at front. The seventeenth hole is a dogleg right that has a 'gunsight' of trees to negotiate from the tees. All along the fairway's right is a huge bunker, part of which has to be carried by tee shots. This bunker also

Hole	1	2	3	4	5	6	7	8	9	Out	
Gold	395	435	544	411	215	430	398	136	584	3548	
Blue	380	412	522	395	186	412	373	127	561	3368	
White	363	389	488	372	162	385	352	112	498	3112	
Red	334	366	471	336	140	321	322	73	463	2826	
Par	4	4	5	4	3	4	4	3	5	36	

Hole	10	11	12	13	14	15	16	17	18	In	Total
Gold	400	383	525	184	460	405	187	400	560	3504	7052
Blue	371	355	513	168	431	390	170	371	526	3295	3099
White	350	339	480	151	412	374	148	350	495	3099	6211
Red	333	318	443	128	381	347	128	333	452	2863	5689
Par	4	4	5	3	4	4	3	4	5	36	72

impinges upon the green approach, and through the trees to the left, you can see the Atlantic Ocean. The green heads toward the beach, and has a hollow at its right, and a bunker and a tree at its left rear.

The eighteenth hole plays along the ocean, with a split fairway that offers golfers a choice. By going right, you can shave strokes from your score, or you can add quite a few if you make the wrong move. It's a carry over the ocean beach to a landing spot having an island of rough to its left, and the beach to its right. From here you can try another beach carry to the green, which has bunkers and trees where an overflight might go, and a rock outcropping known as Stoddard's Point leading down to the ocean, where a badly aimed ball might find its way.

If you go left, trees on the right of the fairway force you to play wide of the island of rough. Then it's an approach to a green having heavy bunkering on its left, and the rocks of Stoddard's Point and the Atlantic Ocean all along the rear. A superb test of golf for anyone's level of ability.

At right: **The eighteenth green, with the majestic Atlantic Ocean to its left.** *Below right:* **The third green: the lake that figures in play along the left prong of the fairway is clearly in view.**

Meridian International Business Center

Englewood, Colorado USA

Meridian International Business Center is a 1200 acre development that combines commercial, office, research and recreational facilities. Over a mile of frontage on Lincoln Boulevard provides major points of access to freeway and local traffic arteries.

This complex is blended artfully into its natural surroundings, and many of its facilities have scenic views of the on-site 18-hole Jack Nicklaus golf course. The entire development occupies high ground that offers panoramic views of the mountains and major portions of the Denver metropolitan areas. Extensive landscaping combines with a series of small lakes, the splendid golf course and the natural beauty of the land to make Meridian a unique working environment.

Centennial Airport borders Meridian on the north. This airport is one of the fastest-growing airports in the country, and is tailored for executive travel requirements. Meridian is home to the new regional headquarters for Toyota Motor Company. Hewlett-Packard is currently designing a seven-state regional training facility for its 14-acre parcel at Meridian, and Teleport Denver has started Colorado's first teleport in Meridian's northern corner.

The 18-hole Jack Nicklaus championship golf course is exclusively for the use of Meridian owners and tenants. With varying tee settings, the yardage on this course stretches from 5983 at the front tees to 7243 at the back tees. The following is a hole-by-hole tour of this classic links-style course.

Hole number one has a cluster of bunkers on the right of the green approach, and another cluster of bunkers on the left of same that stretch along the left of the green. The second hole has a small green that is tightly enclosed by bunkers. Hole number three is a par three that curls around a lake; all but shots from the inner tees face a lake carry to a green that has a bunker on the right and the lake to the left.

The fourth hole is a dogleg left, with a strategically placed bunker on the fairway's right. The tricky green has a bunker on its left. Hole number five has a forked fairway — the left fork avoids the bunkers fronting the green that you meet on the right fork, but at the cost of an extra stroke, it's not much of an advantage.

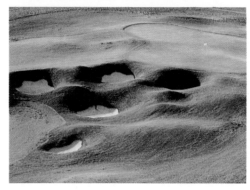

Hole number six is, at 593 yards from the back tee, the longest hole on the course, and is predominately straight with a green that is canted to the right. The green has bunkers on both sides and at rear. A lake lies on the right of the green approach, and on the right and rear of the green. The seventh hole features a wide variety of tee settings, at least one of which features a lake carry. A line of bunkers guards the left of the dogleg right fairway, while the lake is present all along its right. The green is narrow, with bunkers on either side, and with the lake along its right rear.

Hole number eight is a par three that has a lake all along its right, and features lake carries from all but the inner tee. A bunker on the right of the narrow green adds to the challenge here. The ninth hole has a lake on the right of the tees, and a bunker on the

Above left: **Meridian's west perimeter: holes thirteen and fourteen are to the left.** *At left:* **Bunkers at the fifth green.** *Above right:* **Golfers on practice green number two.** *Below:* **A threesome faces the challenge.**

Below left: **Lining up a putt on the fifteenth green.**
Above left: **A lone golf cart negotiates a cart path through the Meridian golf course—here cloaked, by the low sunlight, with an appropriate mantle of gold.**

Hole	1	2	3	4	5	6	7	8	9	Out	
Gold	440	397	167	430	400	593	430	214	549	3620	
Blue	401	339	149	375	335	505	379	190	482	3155	
White	369	310	106	367	326	494	365	175	468	2980	
Red	349	277	88	335	308	478	308	141	439	2723	
Par	4	4	3	4	4	5	4	3	5	36	
Hole	**10**	**11**	**12**	**13**	**14**	**15**	**16**	**17**	**18**	**In**	**Total**
Gold	359	549	454	592	418	201	422	174	454	3623	7243
Blue	319	504	406	575	380	150	362	165	416	3277	6432
White	303	473	369	483	361	136	349	136	366	3003	5983
Red	302	444	290	442	308	136	312	104	301	2639	5362
Par	4	5	4	5	4	3	4	3	4	36	72

landing area. Additional bunkering "is cannily placed on the right of the green approach and on the right of the mouth of the three-sided green.

Hole number ten is a dogleg right, with bunkering all along the right, and the left rear, of the green. The eleventh hole is a dogleg left with a lake fronting the green, and bunkers on all other sides of the green. Golfers at the back tees of hole number twelve face a carry over a stream, which stream then flows to the left of the fairway and the green. Bunkers at left and at right rear of the green, and the arm of a stream on the right of the green, add to the challenge here.

The thirteenth hole is just one yard shorter than the sixth, and a stream that meanders across the green approach necessitates a carry. The green has bunkers in front and along the right side, with the stream also flowing on the right. Hole number fourteen is a dogleg left with part of a stream at the left rear of the green. The fifteenth hole is a par three with a green that lies between the branches of a forked stream. Bunkers at front and rear add to this unusual challenge.

The sixteenth hole has a stream flowing along the left of its tees. This hole is a sharp dogleg right, with a pond all along its inner curve—including the right side and the rear of the green. Hole number seventeen is a par three with part of a lake wrapping around from right rear to the left of the tees, where it forms a stream that meanders on around in front of the tees and continues past the right side of the green. The green has heavy bunkering on its right and left, and its oblique lie makes it a challenge of accuracy.

The eighteenth hole features a stream carry to a narrow fairway that has the stream all along its right. The green has a cluster of bunkers at its left front, and the stream to its right. It's a great finish for eighteen holes of superb golf.

Morningside Golf Course

Rancho Mirage, California USA

Morningside Golf Course is part of The Club at Morningside. The history of this development began in 1980, when Rancho Mirage Joint Venture purchased an $11 million plot of land from Fleetwood Garner, a long-time area resident and aviation enthusiast whose private airstrip once occupied the purchased land.

The name 'Morningside' was derived from a good man and his memories. The much-loved John R 'Jack' Clark gave his time and talents to many civic and philanthropic organizations throughout the Coachella Valley, always putting the needs of others first.

When coaxed into one of his rare recountings of his own life, he always expressed a special fondness for his alma mater, Columbia University. The central focus of his student life had been the campus thoroughfare, Morningside Drive.

Thus, as a tribute to Jack Clark, who gave so much to his neighbors and his community, civic leaders decided to change the name of Thompson Road to Morningside Drive. From that honorable appellation, The Club at Morningside takes its name.

Morningside is a 'signature' community of 375 luxury homes that are part of a residential project that also encompasses 18 lakes and the only Jack Nicklaus-designed golf course in the area. Morningside also includes full tennis facilities and a $10 million clubhouse that includes full amenities.

The Jack Nicklaus-designed Morningside Golf Course has an unusual feature—a contingency hole. Sometimes, the nearby Whitewater River rises, making the regular thirteenth hole unplayable. Therefore, Mr Nicklaus designed a 'contingency' thirteenth, to make the course playable regardless of the state of the river.

In addition to this, the architect's reverence for the classic Scottish course designs to be found in such fabled courses as Old St Andrews, has resulted in features like the double greens to be found at holes four, six, twelve and eighteen, and the pot bunkers that come into play throughout the course. Twenty acres of flowerbeds and 20 acres of water are woven through this course that totals 6816 yards from the back tees. Raised fairways and expansive, rolling greens add yet more distinction to this fine desert course.

A hole-by-hole description of this excellent new golf course follows. Hole number one plays along an irregular fairway to a green that has bunkers on either side. On the fairway's right is a long, broad bunker that this hole shares with hole number nine. The second hole is, at 536 yards, the second longest on the course. Golfers at the tees here face a long lake carry to a landing spot between two huge bunkers. Then it's a carry over rough to a lengthy green approach. The green has a bunker on the right front, and will cause you to exercise your putting skills.

Hole number three is a par three, and features a lake carry from all tees. The green has the lake in front and two bunkers on its right, just where overflights will find them. The fourth hole is a sharp dogleg right, with a lake all along its right-hand side, and a waterfall babbling beside the tees. The lake figures in a carry from the back tees, and the green approach curves so sharply around the other end of the lake that this, too, is a lake carry. The green has a bunker on its left, the lake on its left and a very large bunker—with an island of rough in its center—to the rear.

The fifth hole has a long carry over rough from the tees. A lake and a large bunker to the left could foil your shot if you don't judge it correctly. On the left again is another lake, which flows along the fairway and on past the green. The green has one large bunker at right, and one small bunker on the left, and, of course, water all along its left.

Below: **The island green of Morningside's fifteenth hole.** *At right:* **The beautiful, flower-bedecked waterfall that distracts golfers at the fourth tees.**

Hole number six features a bunker on the left nearing the landing area, and a long carry over rough to a well-bunkered green. The seventh hole is a par three carry over rough to a strategically bunkered green. It demands good judgement and accuracy. Hole number eight is a long dogleg right with a lake carry from the tees and a large bunker on the right of the fairway, to catch overflights. There is lake all along the left, and the green has bunkers on the left approach, on the right and right rear. Here, it all comes down to water and sand.

The ninth is a dogleg right with a long carry over rough to a fairway that has a long bunker on its inner curve. The green requires a good carry on the approach, and is nearly surrounded by bunkers. It's a good, challenging test.

A lake is close by the right side of the tenth hole's tees, and figures a carry from the back tees. Both the distraction of its presence and the real possibility of mis-hitting the ball makes this lake an outstanding challenge. All carries to this fairway are long, and an impinging bunker on the left forms one half of a 'gunsight'—the other half being a large, long bunker to the right. The fairway is split by a wide swath of rough, and re-commences at the green approach with a monstrous bunker on its right, all the way up the side of the green. On the left rear of the shallow, obliquely-set green is another bunker.

The eleventh hole features a carry over the other side of the monstrous bunker that you encountered at the tenth green. The fairway is contoured, and has a massive, long bunker along its right side. The green approach is a carry over rough and the tip of a lake, to a green that has the lake on its right and at rear, and has a bunker at left rear, to catch overflights.

Hole number twelve is a par three with a lake carry to a green that has bunkers everywhere but at rear, and has water at right, front and left. The thirteenth hole is actually two holes—the regular and the alternate, as we have discussed at the beginning of this course description. The regular thirteenth is a dogleg right with bunkers guarding the landing area, and a large bunker all along the left of a rolling green. The alternate thirteenth is a par three (not listed in our yardage table) that features a carry over a huge bunker to a green that has that same bunker guarding its entire left side, front to rear.

Golfers at the tees of hole number fourteen face a long carry to a fairway that has a dozen bunkers all along its right side, and three longitudinal bunkers on the left. The green is protected by two strategically-placed bunkers at left rear and one at right.

At right: **Part of the huge double green shared by the twelfth and eighteenth holes. Palm trees add a Southern California touch to such Scottish features.**

The fifteenth hole is a dogleg left with a long carry over rough from the back tee, a contoured fairway and an island green set in a lake. With bunkers right and left and water everywhere, this lake carry feels like a championship in and of itself. A great test of golfing skill.

Hole number sixteen is, at 196 yards, the longest par three on the course. The green is extremely well bunkered, and if all that sand in front doesn't impress you, the small bunker behind the green is likely to be the depository for overflights. The seventeenth is a lake carry from the back tees, and bunkers lining the

right side will stop most overflights and hooked balls. The lake along the left will also serve to distract golfers trying to concentrate on the green approach, which is a carry over a line of bunkers. The green is expansive and rolling—a good test of putting skill.

The eighteenth hole is a grand conclusion to 18 holes of superb golf. At 568 yards, it's the longest hole on the course. Golfers at the tees of this double dogleg right face a long carry over rough to the first part of a segmented fairway. Then it's another carry to a playing area that has a massive bunker, containing two grassy islands, all along the left. The green approach is engulfed by sand, and the tip of a lake also figures in this intimidating carry to an extremely well-protected green.

At left: **An overview of the fourth fairway and the double green shared by holes four and six.** *Below opposite:* **Part of the eighth fairway and green.** *Below:* **The twelfth and eighteenth double green.**

Hole	1	2	3	4	5	6	7	8	9	Out	
Championship	389	536	155	365	430	424	185	502	393	3379	
Regular	344	482	138	354	379	396	160	491	355	3099	
Senior	328	465	130	302	325	382	152	441	340	2865	
Women's	302	419	125	299	318	351	135	424	310	2683	
Par	4	5	3	4	4	4	3	5	4	36	
Hole	10	11	12	13	14	15	16	17	18	In	Total
Championship	507	390	193	386	410	375	196	412	568	3437	6816
Regular	481	347	156	362	382	361	171	381	557	3198	6297
Senior	467	330	128	338	348	335	158	337	465	2906	5771
Women's	427	318	109	326	330	295	135	317	461	2718	5401
Par	5	4	3	4	4	4	3	4	5	36	72

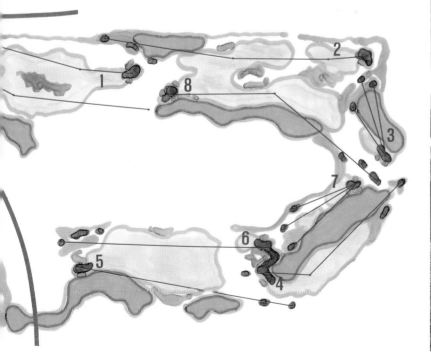

Park Meadows Country Club

Park City, Utah USA

Park Meadows is a luxurious, year-round resort facility and golf course nestled in Utah's picturesque Wasatch Mountains. Magnificent custom homes, townhouses and cottages are tucked around and within the spectacular Jack Nicklaus-designed championship golf course.

The four seasons of the region — the colors, climate, attitudes and activities — are highlighted at the Racquet Club at Park Meadows, where enclosed or open-air tennis, swimming, racquetball and meeting facilities are offered. The region's dry winter snows attract downhill, deep powder and cross-country skiers of all abilities.

Horseback riding, fishing, water skiing, hiking, jogging, backpacking and hunting round out the year. The subtler pleasures await

Below: **The double green of Park Meadows' holes number two and eight. The Wasatch mountains rise up behind this course, named in 1987 as Utah's best.**

you here, too — wildflowers, warm sun, clean air, and enough room to have some solitude when you want it. The resort is near the historic town of Park City, training home of the US Olympic Ski Team, where mining-era buildings impart a rustic charm to the town's many fine amenities.

Also, 30 minutes away is Salt Lake City, with all the excitement and metropolitan activities you could possibly want. Of course, this historic metropolis has as its centerpiece the dramatic and historic Mormon Tabernacle, spiritual center for Mormons around the world. Salt Lake City International Airport is, of course, the region's gateway to the world, and Park Meadows is a scant 40 minutes from this world-class airport.

For our purposes, the Jack Nicklaus-designed golf course. Its high Alpine setting and the changing seasons of the area provide a dramatic backdrop for this fine course, nomi-

nated in the October 1987 issue of *Golf Digest* as the best golf course in Utah.

Park Meadows is a Scottish-style course, with pot bunkers and grass bunkers, a double green (at holes two and eight), firm fairways and treeless fairways. On the other hand, there is also American-style bunkering, sand bunkers, superbly conditioned tee boxes and Pete Dye-style tiered greens — plus three miles of cart paths. September is said to be the best month for golf here. Head pro Don Branca (named by the PGA as Utah's Top Pro of the Year in 1987) is quoted in *Golf Digest* as saying, 'It's warm and gorgeous here that time of year....' It's also the time that the course's 1200 condominiums are available, as the ski season tends to fill them.

The greens are large and possess undulating rolls that portend a real test of putting skill; the fairways arc and are gracefully bent, so that they're hard to 'hold.' Water presents a real challenge on no less than 11 holes. It's treacherous. The greens are surrounded by deep, menacing sand bunkers and at least a few grass bunkers. Quoted in *The Park Record* sports edition, Don Branca says that the bunkers around the greens '... have a way of grabbing iron shots.'

The following is a hole-by-hole description of this excellent course. The first hole is a gentle dogleg right with bunkers on either side of the fairway and a strategically-placed bunker on the right front of the green. The second hole is a very long par four, and has the number one handicap rating on the course. With treacherously-placed bunkers on the right and bunkering on the left, your shot must be straight, long and true. The huge double green presents a putting challenge, and is surrounded with craftily-emplaced bunkers.

The scenic vistas at the third hole will distract you. The green has bunkers all along its left, and water all along its right. If you land in the bunker at the rear of the green, it'll be hard to hold on to the green coming out, and all that water awaits your ball. Your concentration is essential on this green shot.

Hole number four is a par three with water on its left and a green that is bunkered left and right, with two sand bunkers and one grass bunker. The large green will be hard to negotiate. The fifth hole has a water carry from the

tees, and its contoured, straightforward fairway has water from its halfway point on in, on the right, and menacing bunkers along the left. The green is extremely heavily bunkered.

The sixth hole has a ribbon of stream winding in front of the back tees along the right side of the fairway and in front of and along the left side of the green, where it turns into a lake and guards the rear of the green as well. To the left of the narrow green approach is a cluster of bunkers, and the water necessitates a carry. The green has bunkers and lots of water where unconsciously-made approach shots will land.

Hole number seven is a par three that has a water carry off the tees, a tricky, tri-lobed green and a grass bunker set on its face in the interior curve there, and sand bunkers set in the two internal curves at rear. Golfers at the eighth hole face a water carry to a fairway that serpentines left and right, back and forth, between bunkers on either side. At 602 yards from the back tees, this is the longest hole on the course, and it will play long. The green is set obliquely to the left, with plenty of bunkers to protect it.

The ninth hole is a dogleg left, with a bit of playing surface set off to its left, like an island, tempting golfers to take this more direct route to the green. Beware — a bunker lurks in the middle of this 'stepping-stone route.' A bunker lies to the right of the main fairway, and the green is well-protected.

Hole number ten is a serpentine that has bunkers strategically set around the landing area. The large green has bunkers left and right. The eleventh hole is a short and extremely beautiful — but very challenging — hole, and could well become, with the fifteenth, one of this course's 'signature' holes. Number eleven is straight out of Scotland, and has been deemed by golf writer Dave Adler as 'the Valley of Sand.' The tees face a fairway which narrows down a tunnel of bunkers to the left. Due to the high altitude of the course, balls travel farther, and an iron off the tees will bring you to the green approach. Then it's a carry over extensive bunkering to a well-bunkered green.

Hole number twelve is a par three with an irregular green that has a massive bunker on its left and two smaller — but no less threatening — bunkers on its right. The thirteenth hole has bunkers all along the right of the green approach, and the green has bunkers on both sides and at front left.

The fourteenth hole is a dangerous par three, which features a carry over water from the tees. In back of the green, a slope will catch overflights. From this slope, it's practically impossible to get down on the green without rolling into the water. The fifteenth hole is one of the most demanding on the course. It has a narrow fairway with out-of-

bounds stakes on the left and water on the right, with a bunkered, little island fairway off to the right — for those hardy few who want to try for a low score by this precarious route. It's water everywhere, with a green carry from the main fairway that is protected by a bunker at left and water in front of the green. The green has bunkers around it and water in front.

Hole number sixteen plays along a serpentine fairway that has an extremely well bunkered green and green approach. It's not a hole to be taken lightly. The seventeenth hole features a water carry off the back tees, and has treacherous bunkering early on, and the green and green approach here are practically smothered in bunkers.

The eighteenth hole also has a water carry from the back tees, and the fairway is protected right and left with bunkers near the landing area. The green is guarded by copious bunkering at rear and right front. This hole is a great and enjoyable conclusion to an impeccable test of golfing skill.

Hole	1	2	3	4	5	6	7	8	9	Out	
Championship Blue	466	465	444	220	544	363	200	602	472	3776	
Men's White	436	420	404	167	488	331	187	553	432	3418	
Ladies' Red	386	358	374	148	441	283	152	505	338	3035	
Par	4	4	4	3	5	4	3	5	4	36	

Hole	10	11	12	13	14	15	16	17	18	In	Total
Championship Blue	403	401	209	412	189	541	426	502	479	3562	7338
Men's White	343	371	173	390	160	502	379	479	451	3248	6666
Ladies' Red	300	345	136	352	116	466	327	396	343	2781	5816
Par	4	4	3	4	3	5	4	5	4	36	72

Ptarmigan Golf & Country Club

Fort Collins, Colorado USA

Ptarmigan gets its name from a pheasant-like bird that inhabits the higher elevations of the Rocky Mountains. This golf and country club is a unique residential community that is located in picturesque northern Colorado. Quiet elegance is the keynote struck by this fully-equipped course site. Tennis, swimming and a full-service clubhouse featuring fine dining are among the attractions here.

The exciting and challenging Jack Nicklaus golf course, upon which this development centers, is built on land that was bought by a group of local investors in 1979. At that time, Jack Nicklaus was brought in to do the design, and soon thereafter, construction started. The high interest rates of the early 1980s caused a halt in the proceedings, however. Local developer Jim Tull eventually decided that the stoppage had gone on long enough, and in conjunction with Jim Dobbins and his associates, brought the course to completion, with the front nine opening for play in June, 1988, and the back nine opening in the fall of the same year.

Mr Nicklaus has imparted a Scottish flavor to the course at Ptarmigan. Water comes into play on at least 12 holes, holes four and eight have a double green and the greens in general are large and undulating. There are over 100 sand bunkers, some measuring as much as 150 yards in length.

From the championship tees, the course measures 7300 yards. Average and higher-handicap players at Ptarmigan get a break, though, due to the opportunity to play from the regular tees, which cut the distance by some 700 yards overall.

The enjoyment of playing the course has carried over into the realm of bumper stickers that pun, 'Par Me Again.' The challenge of playing from the championship tees has also found its way into popular parlance, with an alternate—and of course, unofficial—course name finding its way into golfers' vocabularies, namely, 'Pt-Armageddon,' complete with its allusion to Webster's definition as a 'great climactic conflict.'

Golfers from non-mountainous locales should be forewarned that playing this course will not only challenge your skills, but will also make you feel younger, as balls hit at this high elevation will travel farther than those hit

in more down-to-earth locales. The following is a hole-by-hole description of this fine new golf course.

The first hole has a fairway with a long bunker to the right of the landing place, and its large, undulating green has bunkers on the right and left. It's a test of putting skill. Hole number two gives you a chace to limber up your driving, and has treacherously placed bunkers at right and left along the fairway, and the green approach narrows dangerously, with bunkers closing in from both sides. The green is protected by bunkers at rear, right and left. This one serves notice that accuracy is a premium shot value on this course.

The third hole unleashes the furies. The fairway has a bunker on its right, near the landing spot, and its fairway is bisected by a diagonal line of large bunkers. The green lies farther down the approach, with a narrow left side (and the concomitant danger of overflying into the rough), and a bunker all along its right side. Hole number four is a par three that features a water carry from the tees. The green here has treacherous curves, with bunkers strategically placed, so as to make golfers of every level really 'lock in' on their accuracy before addressing this tee shot.

Above: **One of Ptarmigan's several 'water holes.'** *Below opposite:* **The defenses of this hole involve bunkers as well as such natural hazards as trees.**

The fifth hole is, at 585 yards, the second longest on the course, and has bunkers at right and left near the landing place. It's a long drive from there to an extremely well protected green that is set obliquely to the fairway, and has a plethora of bunkers, all of them set in the most challenging locations. Hole number six is the longest par three on the course, and features a long carry from the tees to the green. The green has water on its right, left and all along its rear.

Hole number seven has a water carry from the tees. The fairway has a very threatening bunker on its right that cuts across at the landing area, and on the left is a stream that borders the fairway and the green. Bunkers on either side up front protect the green, and a bunker at left rear adds to the challenge, as does greenery all along the rear, and of course, the water to the left. Water comes into play everywhere at the eighth hole—a water carry off the tees to a fairway that is protected right and left with substantial bunkering sets you up for a water carry on the green approach. The double green (shared with hole

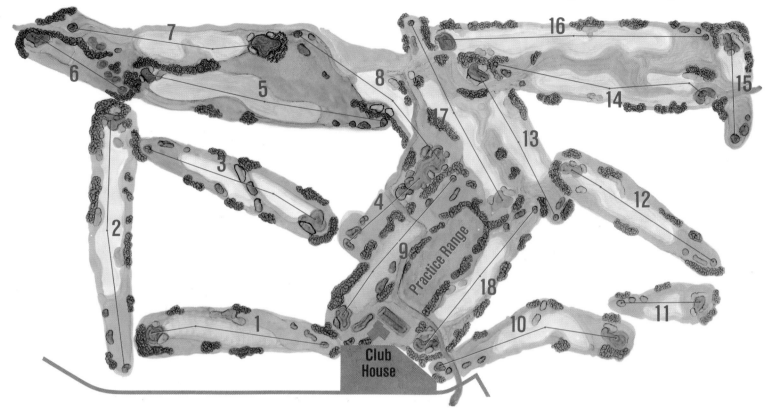

four) has water all along its right, and a massive bunker on its face. Water additionally courses along the left of the fairway.

The ninth hole features a water carry off the tees. The landing spot is hard to hold, situated as it is on a lobe of fairway between two bunkers on the left. The large, undulating green has a bunker at front left, in line with most approach shots, and at right rear, in line with overflights. A great nine going 'out,' and an apt introduction to an equally great nine going 'in.'

Hole number ten is a dogleg right with a stream carry from the back tees. The fairway has a treacherous, hidden bunker on its left, near the landing spot, and an incursion of rough on the right figures in a carry over rough to the large green with a bunker at left front. The eleventh hole is a par three with a green that is practically surrounded by bunkers. This hole demands accuracy and a canny sense of distances.

The twelfth hole is a straightforward hole, with a large bunker cutting into the fairway from the right. On the left of the green approach is another bunker, and on the right front and right side of the green are two more bunkers. It's almost like a pinball game, except that one's ball does not 'bounce off' these defenses. Hole number thirteen is fairly straightforward up to the green approach, which very quickly narrows into a peninsula with huge bunkers on either side and water out front. The green fronts on water and will be a tricky target to hit, and to hold.

Golfers at hole fourteen tee off over water to a serpentine fairway having water all along its left. A bunker haunts the fairway at right, near the landing spot, and water borders it on the

Hole	1	2	3	4	5	6	7	8	9	Out	
Championship	388	569	422	213	585	235	438	460	404	3714	
Regular	368	508	390	183	510	205	390	420	377	3351	
Par	4	5	4	3	5	3	4	4	4	36	

Hole	10	11	12	13	14	15	16	17	18	19	Total
Championship	445	207	385	382	500	223	597	439	402	3580	7294
Regular	420	167	360	362	473	203	547	402	365	3299	6650
Par	4	3	4	4	5	3	5	4	4	36	72

left. Some distance can be cut by means of a water carry to a chunk of fairway to the left. This means another water carry to the green. On the other hand, if you stay on the right-hand fairway, a very long and chancy water carry down the length of the stream is your lot. Either way it's exciting and challenging, and the green has water all along its left side, from front to rear.

The fifteenth hole features a long carry over rough and a stream to a green having bunkers placed strategically all around. The sixteenth is, at 597 yards from the back tees, the longest hole on the course. This is said to be the hardest hole on the course, with a lake running its entire length along the left, and rough to the right. The fairway narrows to 30 yards

at two points, and the green is a difficult target to hit, with bunkers behind and the stream along its left.

Golfers at hole number seventeen must make a water carry to a serpentine fairway that has a large bunker on the left near the landing spot. The green is large and bunkered on both sides in front. The eighteenth hole is straightforward, with bunkers threatening from the right. The green approach is a water carry to a dangerously bunkered green. This is a well-won finale to a spectacular 18 holes of golfing challenge.

Below: **The fifteenth, a demanding par three.** *Bottom, below right and at right:* **A selection of the Rocky Mountain vistas to be had at Ptarmigan, where the altitude will add unexpected yardage to your drives.**

The Country Club of the Rockies

Vail, Colorado USA

The Country Club of the Rockies is a new, Jack Nicklaus-designed golf course which forms the nucleus of the Vail Valley's newest fully-planned recreational community, Arrowhead at Vail. This community features golf as its premier summer activity, with skiing as its premier winter activity. Hosting potential golfers and skiers is the Village at Arrowhead, which features an elegant variety of shops and restaurants, guest accommodations and convenient condominiums.

Visitors and guests are treated to sweeping vistas of beautiful mountain surroundings and the spectacular golf course, plus plazas, walkways and bridges over picturesque McCoy Creek, which winds through the complex. Skiers venturing forth from Arrowhead will find their thrills and challenge either at Beaver Creek or Vail, both of which are ski facilities of international renown.

Golfers will find that their balls travel farther in the thin, high-altitude air at The Country Club of the Rockies than at lower altitudes, and the result will be an increase in vigorous play. Mr Nicklaus designed the course to take full advantage of its natural surroundings—resplendent vistas provide aesthetic pleasure and a challenging distraction on many of the holes here.

Above: **The twelfth green, looking back across the Eagle River and up the fairway.** *Below:* **The twelfth green in play, as seen from the opposite bank.** *At right:* **A beautiful Country Club of the Rockies vista.**

Meticulously manicured greens and fairways are bordered by rolling grass mounds, and, as in the Scottish courses that Jack Nicklaus loves, brooks (called 'burns' in Scotland) run throughout the course, giving an added air of naturalness—and challenge. Overlooking the course is a 24,000 square foot clubhouse that provides year-round recreational and social activity.

The following is a hole-by-hole description of this fine new course. Hole number one is a dogleg left with a big collection bunker on its 'knee.' The green is heavily bunkered on either side of its narrow face, and broadens to the left rear. The second hole has a twin fairway, and the tip of a stream running in from the right figures in a carry from the back tees. Staying to the right will save some distance at the risk of a carry over rough and a crescent of bunkers fronting the green against the right-hand approach. The left fairway is bunkered on its left in such a way that tee shots to the left are jeopardized, but the approach to the green from this fairway is not quite as intimidating as is the approach from the right.

Hole number three is a long dogleg left, which has water all along its inner curve and has a stream running across the fairway in such a way that it's either a long second shot on the fairway, or a long, chancy carry to the green. The green is bunkered at left front, all along the right, and behind. To the left of the green is lots of water.

The fourth hole is the longest par three on the course, and features a long, risky water and bunker carry from the back tees to a well-protected green. This hole is medicine to 'get the cobwebs out,' and sets the tone for challenges to come. Hole number five is a dogleg

right with a very threatening array of bunkers all around the landing spot. Also, all along the right side is a lake, and a long, crescent bunker guards the right side of the green approach, which features—for the more valorous golfers—a carry over a tip of the lake.

The sixth hole has a stream carry from the back tees, and bunkers threaten the landing area from the right. The three-sided green is set edge-on, with a cluster of bunkers on its left face, and a large bunker at right rear. You've got to be on target here. Hole number seven is a dogleg right, with heavy bunkering on the green approach. It's a carry over a veritable valley of sand to the green, which has a strategically-placed bunker on its left

front, and has the tip of the huge bunker, mentioned earlier, on its right.

The eighth hole is a par three with a prodigious lake carry to a green with bunkers at its rear. The ninth hole also features a long lake carry from the back tees, has a stream all along its right and culminates in an extremely well bunkered green. The tenth hole has heavy bunkering on either side of the fairway near the landing area. On either side of a green that widens toward the rear are two additional bunkers.

Hole number eleven tees off across a swale to a green with bunkers right and left, the latter of which figure in the carry from the back tees. The right-hand bunkers are dan-

gerous to overflights from the back tees, and equally threaten mis-hit balls from the forward tees.

Holes twelve, thirteen, fourteen and fifteen play back and forth across the Eagle River. The twelfth hole plays to a serpentine fairway with the river running across the green approach. Golfers at the thirteenth hole must tee off across the Eagle River. This hole is a dogleg right, and it may be hard holding the fairway on the back tee shots. The river is all along the fairway's and green's left, and the green is well bunkered. Hole number fourteen features a carry across the Eagle River to an irregularly-shaped green that is surrounded by bunkers.

Hole number fifteen plays back across the Eagle River to a fairway that is lined on both sides with bunkers. The green has bunkers placed around it to increase the challenge there. The sixteenth hole is a dogleg left with bunkers across the green approach, and the green will test your putting ability.

Hole number seventeen is, at 586 yards, the longest hole on the course. At the landing area, bunkers and stream figure in a carry to the green approach, which is itself another stream carry to a very cannily bunkered green. The eighteenth hole is a dogleg right with a long lake carry from the tees. A bunker lies to the left of the landing area, and the green is very heavily bunkered. This hole will test all facets of your game, and is a superb finish for 18 holes of outstanding golf.

At right: **Morning at the clubhouse. This 24,000 square foot facility overlooks the brilliant course layout and its awesome Rocky Mountain surroundings.**

Hole	1	2	3	4	5	6	7	8	9	Out	
Tournament Green	453	389	566	209	429	427	571	162	400	3606	
Back Blue	428	362	509	168	393	387	352	154	365	3298	
Member White	388	343	473	153	381	352	495	139	325	3049	
Front Red	348	290	405	135	346	322	444	118	288	2696	
Par	4	4	5	3	4	4	4	5	3	4	36
Hole	10	11	12	13	14	15	16	17	18	In	Total
Tournament Green	446	180	477	573	156	415	463	586	415	3711	7317
Back Blue	401	163	413	536	142	401	444	530	369	3399	6697
Member White	365	137	367	439	135	322	418	488	318	2989	6038
Front Red	342	119	327	377	119	302	391	426	287	2690	5386
Par	4	3	4	5	3	4	4	5	4	36	72

Shoal Creek

Birmingham, Alabama USA

Located in central Alabama, in the beautiful valley between Oak and Double Oak mountains, the Shoal Creek golf course is the product of a man's lifelong dream. Hall Thompson, a dealer in tractors and heavy equipment, well known for his commitment to civic duty, had long cherished this dream, and it began to come to fruition when he obtained an option on 1500 acres of central Alabama forest land from a friend of his.

After considering a number of golf course designers, Mr Thompson and his associates settled on the Jack Nicklaus firm, saying they were impressed by the organization's 'exceptional depth.' On Christmas Eve, 1974, Jack Nicklaus called Hall Thompson with the results of a land survey he had done on the area. He felt that the site would justify two golf courses. Mr Thompson felt, however, that one golf course was all that was needed, and so development began on a single golf course that was 'something very special,' in Mr Thompson's words.

The course rises out of the landscape as if it had always been there, waiting to be discovered for golf. The setting is almost overwhelming in its richness and beauty. The stream known as Shoal Creek meanders

Above: **The ninth and eighteenth greens, and the tenth and fourteenth tees, with lakes.** *Below:* **Hole number one, in a vista from the green to the tees.** *Opposite, counterclockwise from the top:* **views of holes five and fifteen; overviews of holes three and six.**

across the valley floor. Its waters, and those of its tributaries, come into play on more than half the holes, and the surrounding natural flora includes oak trees, oakleaf hydrangea, dogwood trees, sourwood trees, maple trees, mountain laurel, native hollies and the full range of pines that grow in Alabama.

Wildlife is equally part of the setting. Early mornings and late afternoons find deer roaming the course at will, and golfers often see wild turkeys foraging in the brush just beyond the fairways. The lakes that were formed by damming Oak Creek in various locations are stocked with bass and bream, and can be fished by club members.

Rare for a course in America's Deep South, Oak Creek has bentgrass greens, which are kept in good condition by a special, finely modulated misting system. The use of bentgrass for the greens here guarantees tournament-level putting surfaces.

Quite amazing—and indicative of the high quality of this excellent course—just seven years after its opening, in 1977, Shoal Creek hosted the 66th PGA Championship in August of 1984. That tournament was a rousing success, and the quality of golf that the course afforded was exceptional. Shoal Creek will host the 72nd PGA Championship in 1990. In 1986 Shoal Creek set another milestone for itself when it hosted the 86th US Amateur Championship.

Honors heaped upon this course include its listing as one of *Golf Magazine*'s '100 Greatest Courses in the World.' *USA Today*'s '130 Best-Designed Golf Courses in the USA' for 1984 listed Shoal Creek as the only Alabama course on that roster. *Golf Digest* included Shoal Creek on its 'America's 100 Greatest Courses' list.

The following is a hole-by-hole description of this truly great young course. Most of the holes at Shoal Creek are tree-lined, which adds splendor and drama to your game. Hole number one plays to a narrow landing area with a large bunker on its left. The green has a large bunker at front left, and this will figure in shots to the green, which is small and very puttable. The second hole is a dogleg right that requires a stream carry from the tees. The large and undulating green is set diagonally to the fairway, hiding its left edge behind a large bunker on its left. The stream accompanies

the fairway for most of its length on the right.

Hole number three plays as a double dogleg unless your tee shot is unusually long and accurate. Bunkers to the left of the average landing area, and a large bunker to the right, on the green approach assure this. The long, narrow green has two bunkers on its right, and one large bunker on its left. Hole number four plays straightaway to a plateau green, and there are no bunkers on the course. This green is almost 10,000 square feet in size, and features unusually interesting pin placement. It has been said that this is one of the finest holes in North America, and will surely challenge you to make par.

The fifth hole is the first par three on the course, and is one of the most photogenic. In autumn, this hole is stunning, as it is played downhill, into a mountain backdrop that comes ablaze with the change of season foliage of the many deciduous trees in the area. A small pond in front of the green, and a large bunker all along the right of the green, make this one a challenge indeed. Jack Nicklaus is quoted in the Shoal Creek PGA Championship publicity booklet for 1984 as saying that the sixth hole at Shoal Creek '… will stand up to any par five that I've ever seen or played for all the qualities needed in a great par five… .' Shoal Creek meanders across the fairway in front of the tees and across the green approach. The green is slender and subtly undulating, and has bunkers at right, right rear and left rear. It is a challenge that could reward you with a birdie or a bogey.

Hole number seven is well bunkered at the landing area, and is a narrow hallway of trees. The green is deep but narrow, and bunkers on either side will require your utmost in accuracy here. The eighth hole is another par three, and features a small green with water in front and to the left, and bunkers in front and behind. This is the sort of challenge one expects from a championship par three.

The ninth hole is a slight dogleg left, and is one of the toughest challenges on the course. It has bunkering just below the 'knee,' and overflights from the tees will find lots of sand. Also on the right is a lake. The green approach is a carry over another lake, which also protects the entire left side of the green and wraps around to its rear. The bunkers to the left of the green add to the challenge here, as do the trees on the edge of the lake behind it. This is a prize that will be proudly won.

A lake and Shoal Creek on the right, and trees on the left, make hole number ten a narrow driving hole. The green has bunkers at right front and left rear, and the creek at right rear. Three tiers add even more challenge to this green, which allows for a great variety of pin placements. The eleventh has a branch of Shoal Creek winding across its fairway, and the creek itself winding across the green approach and around the green. On the green approach, the creek forms a small lake, and widens until it forms a larger lake on the right and at the rear of the green. Aggressive players can easily find the water here, and pot bunkers that additionally front the green add

challenge, as does the larger bunker protecting the landlocked left of the green, which is a multi-level green like that of hole ten.

The twelfth hole plays from an elevated tee to a narrow fairway that is guarded by trees on the right and a large fairway bunker on the left. The green is long and narrow, with a large bunker on its left. This is a hole for driving accuracy, and a par here will be a reward indeed. Hole number thirteen plays across a valley from hillside to hillside, tee to green. The green is protected with bunkers at right, front and left, and a mis-hit shot here can bring disaster in a variety of forms.

Water in front of and to the left of the tees at the fourteenth hole provides distraction and challenge at the start of this hole. The tees are elevated, and nestle in a grove of trees. The lake is a sure threat to all but very accurate shots, and bunkers lie on the left of the green approach of this dogleg right. A small, well bunkered green makes this a challenge for all levels of play. At hole fifteen, a bunker intruding into the fairway from the left makes this hole play as a dogleg left. A carry to the green across a swath of rough chances the three bunkers lining the green's right side. Beware of the left of the green, however, as it is said that errant shots to this area are more difficult to recover than those that find the bunkers.

Hole number sixteen, a par three, plays downhill in a hallway of trees. The green has

bunkers at front right and at left, and in the rear, a pot bunker and a grass bunker add to the protection and challenge. A dogwood tree in the left bunker adds to the distraction and difficulty of recovering shots mis-hit in that direction. This hole will yield both birdies and bogeys, depending on the attentiveness of each golfer.

The seventeenth hole is called the 'waterfall hole' for the stream configuration that crosses the green approach. Bordered close on either side by dense woodland, and protected earlier on by a bunker on the right, the fairway at this hole will demand your best long shots. A dogwood tree on the left about two-thirds of the way down will come into play for some errant shots. The green is fronted by the

aforementioned waterfall, and has a lake to its left. A bunker guards the right, and trees the rear, while the green's apparently flat surface has several subtle breaks in its center.

Hole number eighteen has a large bunker on the right of the fairway, and trees close by on the left may come into play, as can the lake, which lies to the left along the green approach and along the side of the green, which has additional water along its back. To the right of the green and the green approach is a stream. The green is extremely well bunkered, and is quite large, with a pronounced swale. This will prove to be an outstanding finishing hole for an exciting course that has even just yet begun to garner the honors it so richly deserves.

Hole	1	2	3	4	5	6	7	8	9	Out	
Championship	409	424	530	458	189	554	443	177	428	3612	
Standard	402	417	527	438	189	551	426	161	428	3539	
Par	4	4	5	4	3	5	4	3	4	36	
Hole	10	11	12	13	14	15	16	17	18	In	Total
Championship	415	517	452	177	383	407	197	539	446	3533	7145
Standard	410	492	445	172	381	404	194	504	443	3445	6984
Par	4	5	4	3	4	4	3	5	4	36	72

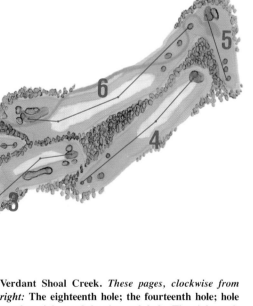

Verdant Shoal Creek. *These pages, clockwise from right:* **The eighteenth hole; the fourteenth hole; hole number eight; and the sixteenth hole. The eighteenth and the fourteenth are essentially joined head to foot, with a line of trees separating the two fairways. Many of these holes play over water.**

New St Andrews Golf Club

Tochigi Prefecture, Japan

Tom Weiskopf is quoted in the New St Andrews brochure as saying that this course is one of the most beautiful and exciting courses he has ever played. Mr Weiskopf goes on to say, 'Come the day when it hosts a major tournament, I believe it will be recognized as one of the greatest golf courses not only in Japan, but in the entire world.'

Jack Nicklaus designed the 18 holes of the 'New Course' at New St Andrews, which fills out the original nine that form the 'Old Course' at New St Andrews. The New Course's 18 holes provide a tremendous variety of shot values. The course is not partic-

ularly hilly, and yet elevation throughout the layout is such that magnificent views are availed to players at every fairway, tee and green.

There are valley holes; hillside holes; open links-like holes; wooded holes; straightaway holes; dogleg holes; and large, double and small greens. It is a course at which you'll have to use every club in your bag. Named for the hallowed course in Scotland, New St Andrews bears the traditional insignia of the eponymous saint, with the distinctive cross upon which he was martyred, and his famous motto, written in Latin: 'Dum spiro spero,'

which is to say, 'While I breathe, I hope.' St Andrew's cross was a mark of his hope and humility—his humility was a mark of his greatness in the eyes of God.

Just so, the greatness of St Andrews in Scotland follows the Scottish *modus operandi* of taking on the forms of humble nature and elevating them to the status of greatness—and this lineage has been passed down through one of the greatest admirers of traditional Scottish golf design, Jack Nicklaus, who has

Below: **The tip of the New Course sixth fairway: to its right, the sixth green. Ahead is the third green.** *At right:* **A blossom-bedecked view of New St Andrews.**

infused New St Andrews with more than a few of the traits of beautiful, and challenging, humility that are to be found in the classic Scottish courses.

Its natural surroundings seem to have always held this course in their contours, and golfing here is the excitement of a serious, but fair, challenge. The following is a hole-by-hole description of the 'New Course' at New St Andrews. Hole number one is a brisk beginning. It's a slight dogleg right, with bunkers on its outer 'knee,' and a lake all along the right side. There's not a lot of room between the bunkers and the lake, and for many, it'll be a water carry to the green.

A lake lies to the right of the second hole's tees, and figures in a carry to the fairway. From the landing area, it's a shot to a green having a massive bunker out front and extensive bunkering behind. A magnificent challenge. Hole number three is one of the most beautiful holes on the course. A semi-blind tee shot should bring you into good position for the shot to the green approach, which for most players will involve laying up before the carry across the tip of the lake to the green, which has bunkers and a hillside at its back. Watch out for that green approach, too—a mis-hit second shot could find the sand to the left or the lake to the right.

Hole number four is a dogleg left, with a green that is surrounded by bunkers. Additionally, the green has a split-level surface with a 'knob' in its middle. It'll be a real test to birdie here. The fifth hole is a par three that plays downhill. Its green has big bunkers guarding either side of its front, and a cherry tree guarding the right third of the green. This can be a very demanding hole. The green at the sixth hole is sandwiched between bunkers on the right and a lake on the left. A bunker also lies behind the green, and mis-hits are likely to find sand or water here.

Hole number seven has an elevated tee and a plethora of bunkers intruding on the fairway from the right. To the left is a hillside. Trees and shrubs additionally challenge all along the right. The green has heavy bunkering in front and behind, but there's a chance for a birdie here. The eighth hole is a par three with a long carry over a lake to a large green with bunkers all along the right and left side. The cant of the green is toward the lake. A truly beautiful challenge.

Hole number nine is an unusual challenge that involves a hogback ridge on the fairway that must be overcome to establish a good stance for the tee shot. The green shot will be semi-blind. You won't see the bunker at front

Clockwise from above opposite: **The eighth hole, from the tees to the green; the seventeenth hole, seen from the tees; the sixteenth green, from the fairway; a greenward view of the par three seventeenth hole; a view of the first fairway from its green.**

Hole	1	2	3	4	5	6	7	8	9	Out	
Blue	442	3376	534	527	207	365	342	179	344	3316	
White	407	346	488	488	187	337	314	162	331	3060	
Red	346	282	470	466	139	314	274	93	265	2649	
Par	4	4	5	5	3	4	4	3	4	36	
Hole	**10**	**11**	**12**	**13**	**14**	**15**	**16**	**17**	**18**	**In**	**Total**
Blue	489	359	538	409	152	464	375	193	428	3407	6723
White	480	310	501	392	131	434	362	159	403	3172	6232
Red	427	268	460	375	102	371	295	125	324	2747	5396
Par	5	4	5	4	3	4	4	3	4	36	72

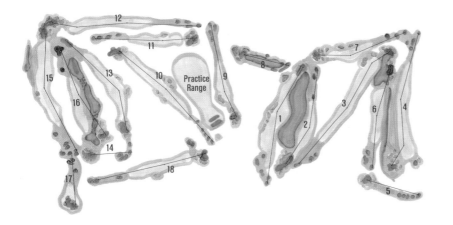

right, for instance, until you've either put your ball in it or on the green. If you overshoot, sand and a hillside await your shot.

At the tenth hole, golfers will tee off across a valley to a landing area that is bracketed with bunkers right and left. The green has bunkers out front on both sides. It's a great start to the 'inbound nine.' At hole number eleven, players are faced with a fairway that has a gully, and has heavy bunkering on the left, and a tree on the fairway, near the green approach. Bunkers at front, left and right guard the large green.

The twelfth hole plays downhill toward a green that is surrounded by bunkers and has a scenic drop-off to the rear. In addition, this is a double green that is shared with the fifteenth hole. Hole number thirteen is a very long-playing par four, with trees and bunkers that lie in the dogleg's outer 'knee.' The green is a split-level surface that is guarded at left front and at right rear with big bunkers. It's a tough hole to play. The fourteenth hole is a par three on which golfers tee off over a valley to a heavily bunkered green with a backdrop composed of a mound of mountain stones and boulders.

The fifteenth is a dogleg right with bunkers and a hillside on its inner 'knee,' and bunkers and a depression on its outer 'knee.' This hole has elevated tees, and plays downhill to a green having one massive bunker on its left front, and bunkering at right and at rear. The green is a double, shared with hole number twelve.

The sixteenth hole seems destined to become one of the most photographed holes in golf. A rippling series of waterfalls runs the entire length of the hole from left to right, cutting across for a spectacular hazard—and distraction—at the green approach. The green is tucked into an amphitheater-like hillside and fronts on the water, and has heavy bunkering at rear and on its exposed left face.

Tee shots at the par three seventeenth hole are severely downhill to an hourglass-shaped green that is protected all around with bunkers. The segment of the green on the left has a hogback ridge, while the right-hand segment is bowl-contoured. This is a very challenging, and potentially decisive, hole. The eighteenth hole is a good, rigorous finish to a spectacular 18 holes of golf. The tee shot should pull up short of going over the top of a hill that fronts the green approach—over the hill is a valley from which it would be very tough to get to the green. The green approach shot should carry over the valley and the intensive bunkering that fronts the green. A hillside lies behind the green.

Above opposite: **A view down the second fairway to the green.** *Below opposite:* **The third green and green approach.** *At left:* **A view from the eighteenth fairway of the eighteenth green and the St Andrews clubhouse.**

St Mellion Golf & Country Club

Saltash, Cornwall England

The much-acclaimed Jack Nicklaus golf course at St Mellion was literally built around the 'Old Course' at St Mellion. The Old Course, designed by J Hamilton Stutt in 1974, was also reworked by the Nicklaus group at the time of the construction of the new Nicklaus course, which opened in August of 1986, and had its official opening in the summer of 1988. Fashioned over a period of three years from a hillside of thick forest and slender river valleys, St Mellion is Great Britain's most 'American' course. This course is a target golf course, and tests a player's hitting length and precision.

The St Mellion Golf & Country Club provides a fleet of buggies, a full time course monitor and PGA qualified staff who operate from the clubhouse. The 'St Mellion Club House' opened in 1976 and was extensively refurbished in 1985, and offers facilities both for leisure and for business; its second floor lounge and leisure area overlooks the eighteenth green of the Nicklaus Course and offers views of Plymouth Sound and Dartmoor.

The restaurant and ballroom both offer views of the rolling Cornish landscape, and offer superb accommodations for quiet, intimate dining or a dinner dance for up to 200. A variety of menus are offered for both restaurant dining and private functions, and an extensive wine list caters to even the most discerning palate. These facilities are available for wedding receptions, golf society meetings and business conferences.

The grill room offers a wide variety of meals from noon to 10 o'clock in the evening, and the coffee shop offers a varied selection of snacks and sweets from 10 o'clock in the morning to 10 o'clock in the evening.

The St Mellion Hotel has eight rooms with double beds and 16 rooms with twin beds, all with private bathrooms, color television, radio, direct dial telephones and child care services. Children are welcome, and can be accommodated free of charge, with meals charged as taken. All guests staying at the hotel are classified as temporary members of the club. Gentlemen staying in the hotel must wear a jacket, collar and tie when using the lounge bar and restaurant facilities after seven o'clock in the evening. All rules pertaining to standards of dress and etiquette on the golf course must be complied with.

In addition to these, St Mellion has accommodations, including a multi-gym, for more than a dozen organized sporting and leisure activities, some of which are squash, badminton, racquetball, table tennis, indoor swimming, sauna, solarium, snooker and tennis. Qualified instructors are on hand for all of the sports, and a full time sports coach is on hand to ensure the smooth running of the sports program. This golfing facility is also the site of 50 timeshare lodges that take full advantage of the beautiful vistas afforded by the Old Course. These lodges can be leased through the Wimpey Time-Ownership Sales Office.

St Mellion's Old Course has itself hosted such events as The Benson & Hedges International Open, the 1983 and 1984 Tournament Players Championship, and five Celebrity Golf Classics. The new Nicklaus Course was built to provide an even more spectacular round of golf at St Mellion, and while the Old Course received some upgrading by the

At right: **A view from behind a tee position of St Mellion's hole number eleven, a par three.** *Below:* **A view down the length of hole six from the green end. This course occupies a verdant Cornish hillside.**

Nicklaus organization, we will now focus on the brilliant Nicklaus Course at St Mellion.

Golf authority Colin Callander is quoted in the St Mellion promotional material as stating, 'In time it will undoubtedly become one of the finest venues in Europe. Just don't expect it to be similar in style to other championship courses around the country... It's a piece of America in the heart of Cornwall.' St Mellion owners Martin and Hermon Bond engaged Jack Nicklaus to build the superb and demanding Nicklaus Course at St Mellion in 1982. The Nicklaus Course was opened in autumn of 1986.

The greens are constructed in the American mode, using peat and sand, and seeded with an American grass to provide a superb putting surface that resists puddling even in wet weather; further, this mode of greens construction provides a very fast and true putting surface that also is able to stop a ball dead from a carefully conceived approach shot. This fine course design also has, as a complement, a Nicklaus-designed practice range.

The Nicklaus Course was also designed to be the best appointed layout for spectators in the world. Every consideration is given to spectators' needs, and vantage points overlook every green of this championship golf course. In the building of this course, Mr Nicklaus worked in contrast to his much-beloved Scottish traditional stratagem for design—ie, letting the course follow the lay of the land, and effecting the difficult transformation from natural landforms to a golf layout that appears to have been created by natural processes, and gives the impression of always having been a local feature.

For St Mellion, the Nicklaus organization had to create the course site out of a difficult hillside. Diggers excavated 1.5 million cubic yards of soil to transform sloping fields into canting fairways, and on many holes you are faced with a fairway with an incline on one side and a steep drop-off on the other. The signature Nicklaus mounding is found throughout the course. Four lakes were created, and water comes into play on half the holes, and the fifth and the twelfth holes are two spectacular examples; on the former, the tee shot has to carry 170 yards of water, and on the latter, water protects the right side of the fairway and then cuts across in front of the green.

Colin Callander says, 'Some holes may not have the exact playing characteristics of Augusta, but somehow they *feel* just like it.' The British Ladies Open has been played at 'the Nicklaus Course,' as has the St Mellion Trophy, featuring Jack Nicklaus, Tom Watson, Sandy Lyle and Nick Faldo. While the European PGA Tour had no immediate plans for the course as of its official opening, Ken Schofield, the Tour's executive director, was quoted in *Golf* magazine of May 1987 as saying, 'The golf course is so good that we will encourage people [sponsors] to go there.'

Playing the course is the real test of its mettle, though, and this course will test your abilities, whatever level of golf you play. Each hole has its own individual character; it's been said that you'll never play the same shot twice. This is a course that rewards your good shots, and penalizes your bad shots. Therefore, the 350-yard practice range will be of great use to you in preparing to play this course. In addition, you can always take a few tips from the resident PGA professional.

The following is a hole-by-hole description of the Nicklaus Course at Saint Mellion Golf

& Country Club. The first hole plays downhill toward an elevated green. This hole is a tough challenge when the weather is absolutely perfect, with rough and trees at right, a downward slope to the left, and a green with a bunker on its left face and one on its right side.

Hole number two has a hillside on its right, and a stream all along its left. The green has bunkers at front left and right. A hillside to the left and a sheer, 100-foot drop along the right of the third hole fairway and green creates a difficult target from this hole's raised tees. The green has a hillside on the left and behind, and a small drop-off preceding the large one discussed above, to its right. Bunkers left and right complete the challenge here.

The fourth hole is a par three, with hillside to the left and drop-off to the right. Bunkers line the right side of the green, which is a mercy—anyone going too far right will meet with disaster. Hole number five is extremely beautiful, and features a 180-yard carry over a lake from the championship tees. Trees on the left place a premium on accuracy here, and the green approach is a stream running along a Cornish-style wall. There's water in front of, and to the left of, the green, a hillside behind and a bunker at right.

Hole number six has a hillside to the left

Below: **A view of the sixteenth green. Note the deep bunkering, and the hillside which lies beyond in this view. Such defenses are typical of St Mellion's.**

and a stream and trees to the right. The green here will test your putting ability. The seventh hole is a dogleg left, with a stream and trees along its left, and a hillside, trees, and the eighth green on its right. The trees on either side close in on the fairway at its 'knee,' and the green has bunkers at left front and right front, with a downhill slope to the stream on its left side.

Golfers at the eighth hole, a par three, must make the carry over a drop-off to a green that has a hillside to its left, and a drop-off to its right. A bunker at left rear, and bunkers along the right side, plus trees at its right rear, complete the defenses around the green. It's a study in perspective that will cause you to consider this tee shot a bit more thoroughly than many other tee shots.

The ninth hole is a dogleg right with a bunker at the bottom of a hollow on the right of the fairway. This bunker will be a carry for most tee shots. The green has a bunker at right front, and there are hillsides all around this hole, creating an 'amphitheater' effect. After these outstanding nine holes 'out,' golfers have the pleasure of taking up the brilliant challenge of the second nine of the Nicklaus Course at St Mellion.

Hole number ten is an outstanding dogleg right, with trees forming a hallway for the tees, and trees on the fairway further stress this hole's emphasis on accuracy. A stream and trees all along the right, and a hillside on the left, add to the constraints here, while the green is backed by a hillside, with trees at right rear. The eleventh hole requires golfers to tee off across a lake. The trees to the right could cause some difficulty in a crosswind, and the bunker at right front of the green will be a problem for golfers who don't quite make the carry. It's a classic challenge.

The twelfth hole features a lake carry from the back tees to a wide, rolling fairway, and the green approach involves a stream that follows the right side of the fairway and then cuts across in front of the green. The green has—in addition to trees on the left—the stream in front and on the left, and a hillside to the right. Hole number thirteen has a hillside to its right, trees on the right of the green approach, and a large bunker and shrubbery on the left. Two bunkers defend the green at front and rear left, and a smaller bunker defends its right side. A cart path cuts across in front of the green.

The back tee at the par three fourteenth hole is set into a hillside; all tees must carry over a cart path valley and fairway bunkering. The green has a hillside to its left and a bunker and trees to its right. Hole number fifteen is a dogleg right with trees along its right-hand side, and trees forming a 'gunsight' for back tee shots. Tee shots here must also carry a ravine. The green has bunkering on either side

and behind, and heads into a hillside. Don't go far left on this fairway, as a drop-off guards that side.

The sixteenth hole is a dogleg left, with bunkers on either side of the fairway early on, and trees along the right of the tees. A hillside lies to the left. At the green approach, a large bunker is set lengthwise in the center of the fairway, and bunkers on either side, set a few yards ahead, seem destined to receive a great many lay-up shots. The green has large bunkers right and left, and a bunker at right rear, plus trees to the right. Hole number seventeen

is a dogleg right, with mounds along its left-hand side, and trees along its right, with at least one tree situated in the middle of the fairway. A cart path cuts across in front of a green that is set into a hillside.

A small lake tucked in below the clubhouse adds color and challenge to the eighteenth hole, a dogleg right with a bunker in its inner 'knee.' Trees line the tees, and mounds line the fairway and green. It's an exciting finish to eighteen holes of great golfing, as you play into the valley toward the green with a lake on its left.

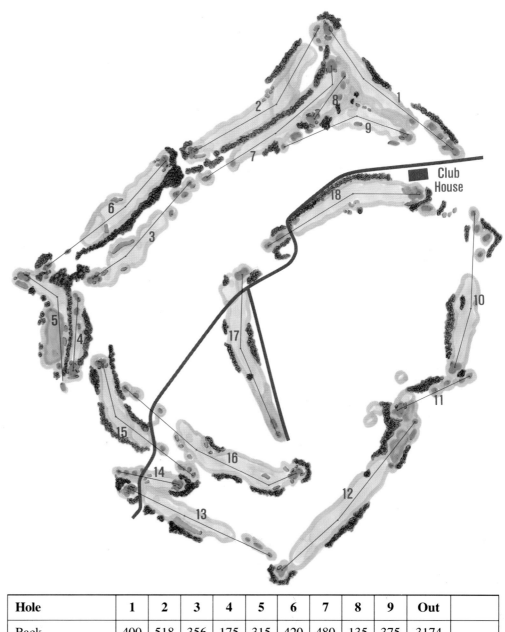

Hole	1	2	3	4	5	6	7	8	9	Out	
Back	400	518	356	175	315	420	480	135	375	3174	
Forward	338	477	300	125	220	360	413	105	330	2668	
Par	4	5	4	3	4	4	5	3	4	36	
Hole	10	11	12	13	14	15	16	17	18	In	Total
Back	410	181	525	361	158	411	520	426	460	3452	6626
Forward	393	103	413	324	125	358	485	346	415	2962	5630
Par	4	3	5	4	3	4	5	4	4/5	36/37	72/73

Sunnyfield Golf Course

Tokyo, Japan

This Jack Nicklaus eighteen hole signature course is replete with wide-open vistas, tree-lined fairways, scenic ridges, and verdant valleys. Lakes adorn this course like liquid jewels, and flowers beautify various course locales.

Scottish influence is evident here: such features as the double green at the tenth and thirteenth holes, and the natural contours of this course are combined with American-style putting surfaces and the wonderful natural contours and greenery of its Japanese locale. The following is a hole-by-hole description of this fine new course.

The first hole has trees to the right of its back tees, emphasizing accuracy in playing to a tree-lined fairway that has heavy bunkering to the left of the landing area, and bunkers cutting into the green approach from the left. A small pond glimmers through the greenery on the left, and may distract you with its disarming allure. You'd best keep your concentration, however, as the crescent bunker on the right of the green, or the trees behind, may cause you to regret not having done so.

Hole number two is a par three with a well bunkered, tree-surrounded green. The third hole is a dogleg right with a large bunker on the left of the fairway, just where overflights from the tees may find it. The green has a pot

Above: **The thirteenth fairway.** *Below:* **The view from the tenth tees.** *At right:* **The eighth green (near) and the seventh green (across the lake). Uphill to the left of the seventh green are the eighth tees.**

bunker on its left front face, and is large and subtly contoured. The back tee of hole number four has to negotiate trees to the right. This hole is a dogleg right with a bunker in its inner 'knee,' and two bunkers to the right of the green.

The fifth hole is a dogleg left with a large bunker stretching along the right of the landing area, and another long bunker stretching along the left of the green approach, bordering half of the green's left side. The narrowness of the forward part of the green causes this bunker to represent a considerable threat. Hole number six is a par three with a well bunkered green.

The green approach of dogleg right hole number seven borders, on the left, the same rock-lined, flower-bedecked lake that figures so prominently in the play at the eighth hole. Hole number seven has bunkers bracketing its 'knee' and green approach. Trees to the right rear of the green, and the lake on the left, add to the drama of this putting green.

Golfers at hole number eight can play it as a dogleg left, at the cost of an extra stroke, or can go for a long lake carry to the green, at the risk of not making the carry. A large bunker across the lake from the tees may be a target for the valorous attempting the lake carry. The green is very well bunkered, and overflights and other mis-hit balls will find a lot of sand to its rear.

The ninth hole is a double dogleg with a bunker on the left of the beginning of the fairway, necessitating a carry for most tee shots. The green approach is squeezed between two longitudinal bunkers, and the irregularly-shaped green has bunkers left and right, and a pot bunker in front.

The tenth hole plays along a serpentine fairway that has a bunker at right near the green approach, and the green is part of a double green shared with hole number thirteen. Bunkers at left and right, with lots of putting surface, complete the playing picture

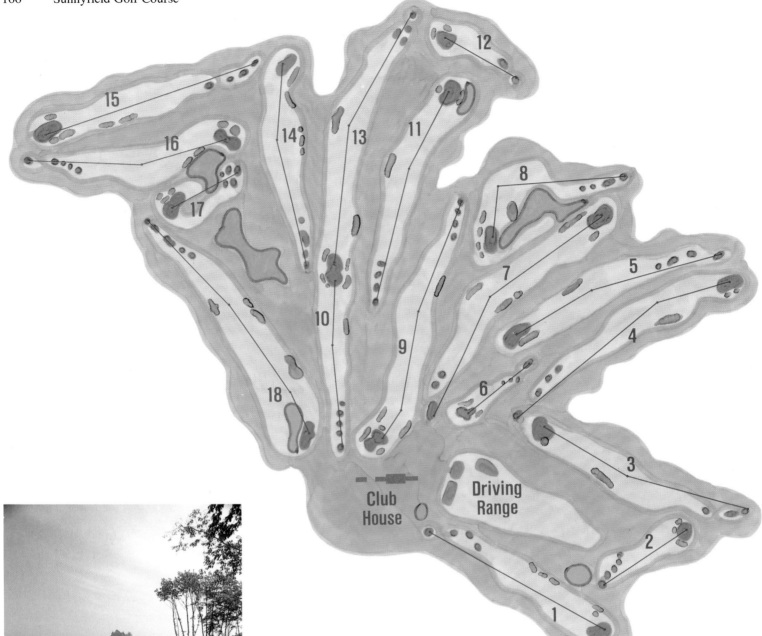

At left: **The serene but challenging seventh hole.** *Above right:* **A perspective of the eighth hole from the green end.** *Below right:* **The seventeenth hole, a beguiling** and challenging par three, as seen from the green. Golfers at this hole's elevated tee boxes are faced with a carry over the lake seen here.

here. Hole number eleven is a dogleg right, with a large bunker on its outer 'knee.' The green is long and narrow, with longitudinal bunkers at right and left, and a pond on the outer perimeter of the right-hand bunker.

A par three, the twelfth hole features a green that will test your putting skills. Backing the green in the center and on the right are bunkers. The thirteenth hole is a dogleg left with a large bunker to the right of the landing spot, where overflights from the tees will find it. A bunker to the left of the green approach guards against mis-hit lay-ups there, and the green is, as we have already mentioned, part of the double green shared with the tenth hole. Bunkers right and left guard this expansive putting surface.

The fourteenth hole is a dogleg right, with a chain of bunkers extending from halfway down the fairway to halfway along the side of

Hole	1	2	3	4	5	6	7	8	9	Out	
Gold	416	196	411	455	446	158	538	323	514	3467	
Blue	398	177	365	442	376	138	515	296	479	3186	
White	348	156	348	399	345	121	508	286	462	2973	
Red	326	105	319	351	316	100	487	226	440	2670	
Par	4	3	4	4	4	3	5	4	5	36	
Hole	**10**	**11**	**12**	**13**	**14**	**15**	**16**	**17**	**18**	**In**	**Total**
Gold	367	443	159	543	421	444	410	174	602	3563	7030
Blue	337	421	133	516	398	417	377	151	574	3324	6510
White	310	405	121	490	368	393	371	141	553	3152	6125
Red	267	359	109	475	303	349	329	120	475	2786	5456
Par	4	4	3	5	4	4	4	3	5	36	72

the green, on the right. The lake gleaming off to the left of the tees at this hole could be a strong distraction. Hole number fifteen has a chain of bunkers all along its left, and a challenging green that has bunkering left and right. The sixteenth hole is a dogleg left with heavy bunkering and a lake pushing into the green approach from the right, and the green has large bunkers on its left. You'd better be attentive on this green approach.

The seventeenth hole is a par three with a lake carry to a kidney-shaped green that wraps around a lobe of the lake. Bunkers guard the right-hand side of this green. Hole number eighteen is, at 602 yards from the championship tee, the longest hole on the course. This driver's delight starts off narrow, with a 'gunsight' of bunkers at the landing spot, and bunkers all along the left. The fairway splits at the green approach, and golfers have a choice of a long lake carry, or an extra stroke and a short water carry. Either way, this is a great way to finish eighteen holes of an extraordinary and enjoyable test of golfing ability.

Below: **The eleventh hole, as seen from across the pond that guards the green.** *Above:* **The fifth hole, seen from its green end.** *At right:* **A view from the tees of the second hole, a sun-dappled par three.**

These pages: A view from the seventeenth tees. This very beautiful Japanese course features brilliant Jack Nicklaus design—calculated to challenge all players.

Valhalla Golf Club

Eastwood, Kentucky USA

Golfers in Kentucky have long desired to have a world-class golf course in their home state. In 1981, the Gahm family commissioned Jack Nicklaus Club Management to conduct a survey on the feasibility of constructing such a facility in the Louisville area. The parameters the Nicklaus organization were given were that the proposed golf club would be small, exclusive, private, for golf only, and would be unmatched in the state of Kentucky.

The name 'Valhalla' is from Norse mythology; Valhalla was the mythic Norse heaven for heroes, where Odin surveyed the domain in the form of a golden eagle. Instead of a golden eagle, however, 'the Golden Bear' will be surveying this domain, through his firm, which has contracted to manage and maintain the facility, so that golfers will enjoy heroically good golfing for years to come.

Not that you have to be a hero to play this course, as variant tee settings enable golfers of every ability to be met on their level with a fair, exciting challenge. Indeed, Jack Nicklaus is quoted in the Valhalla informational packet as saying, 'I don't design courses to suit myself as far as difficulty goes. I design them to match the players who are going to be playing the course.... Golf is a game of precision, not strength... My aim is primarily to test a golfer's accuracy.'

The course incorporates a full range of shot values to test playing skills, and incorporates such Scottish-influenced features as fairway mounding, split fairways and the use of natural landforms and features to shape the course. Members and guests prepare for the demands of Valhalla on a practice area that is designed to parallel the challenges of the course. Golfers at Valhalla will meet such features as an island fairway, a rock quarry, a large island green encircled by boulders and water, 30-50 foot elevated hillside tees, and a very beautiful terraced waterfall.

After playing this excellent course, golfers can relax in the 'Villa' overlooking the tenth green, dine in the 'Great Hall,' or enjoy a quiet game in the card room. The main clubhouse overlooks the eighteenth green, and is designed with a relaxing, classical, lodge-type atmosphere in mind. Villa suites are soon to be available for the comfortable accommodation of members and guests.

Above: **A view from the tees of the eleventh hole, a par three.** *At right:* **A view of the challenging fourth green.** *Overleaf:* **The beauteous and distracting thirteenth green, set on an island in Floyds Fork.**

The following is a hole-by-hole description of this great new golf course. Hole number one is a dogleg left with trees on its inside 'knee,' and mounding along the right of the fairway, the left of the green approach and on three sides of the green. The second hole is a double dogleg left, with a tributary of Floyds Fork running along its left side. The tees face a carry over another branch of the stream, and the fairway is undulating and tree-lined, and has a large bunker somewhat hidden by the trees on the right.

The third hole is the longest par three on the course, and features a carry over Floyds Fork to a green that will test your putting skills. Golfers at hole number four face a carry over mounding to a dogleg left fairway with bunkers on both sides of its 'knee.' Mounds to the right provide a contoured perimeter. The irregularly-shaped green has bunkers on the right and left, and trees behind.

Hole number five is a dogleg right that has mounding all along its right, on both sides of the green approach and on three sides of the green. With a large bunker on its right, this green will test your accuracy. The sixth hole is a long dogleg right, with mounds to the left and Floyds Fork flowing along its right-hand side. The green approach is a stream carry, and the green, with just a small bunker and a rock wall between its front and the water, is

backed with mounds. You'd best be on your game here.

The seventh hole is spectacular. At 603 yards from the back tees, this is a challenge to your driving ability and sense of accuracy. However, it's not an unfair challenge: at the cost of perhaps an extra stroke, you can avoid the physical challenge. It's straight ahead for the hearty—an island fairway is situated in the midst of a rock quarry, and it demands a long carry over a quarry and Floyds Fork from the tees. From this fairway, it's a second long carry, over the rest of the quarry, to a green that is set in a cul-de-sac of mounds. This same hole plays to the right for those who feel less sure of their strength and accuracy. A stream carry brings you to a double dogleg-left fairway that circumvents the quarry. Mounding and strategically placed bunkers (near the green approach) lie to the right, and the green will challenge your putting skills.

Golfers at the par three eighth hole tee off for an oblique carry over Floyds Fork to an island green with trees on its left, a bunker behind—and water beyond the bunker—and a slope to the water on the right. The ninth is a dogleg right with mounding on both sides, a bunker near the landing area, and a bunker on the right of the green. Trees lie behind and on the left of the green.

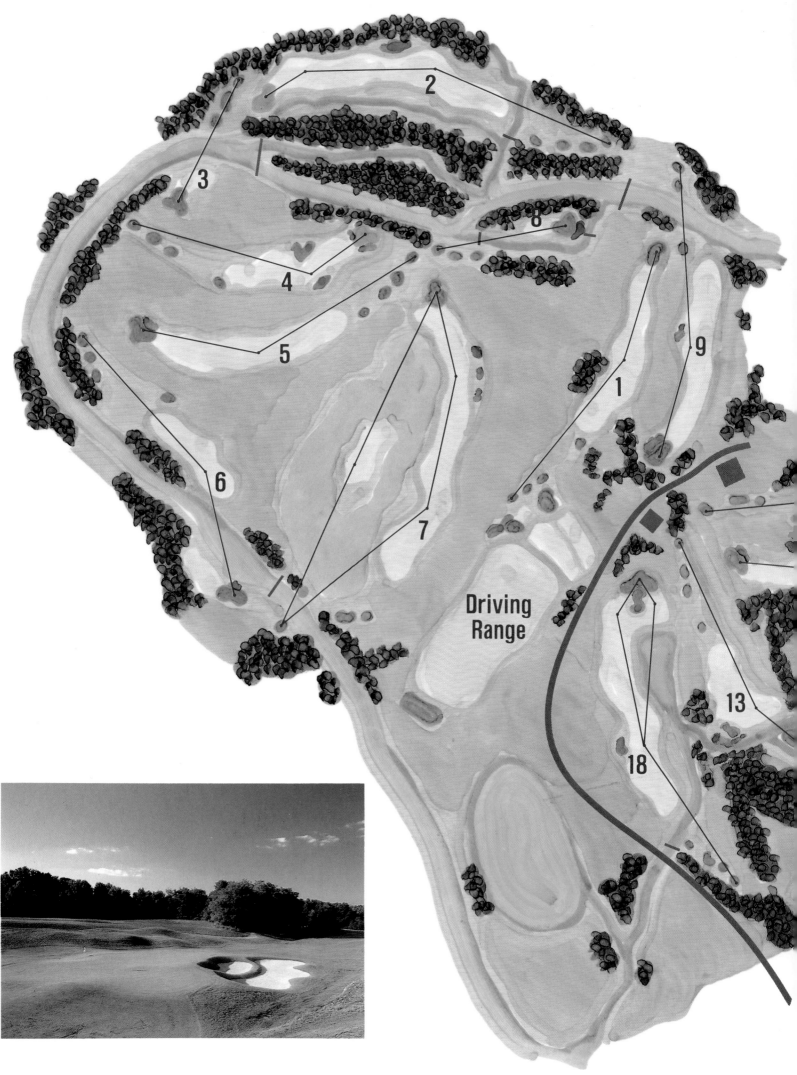

Hole	1	2	3	4	5	6	7	8	9	Out	
Championship	425	511	199	355	459	416	603	164	416	3548	
Blue	381	479	160	315	410	386	530	148	392	3401	
White	347	460	151	282	381	360	507	140	382	3349	
Forward	312	417	112	205	311	270	465	125	302	2519	
Par	4	5	3	4	4	4	5	3	4	36	

Hole	10	11	12	13	14	15	16	17	18	In	Total
Championship	565	165	470	351	188	408	447	409	536	3539	7087
Blue	526	150	435	314	157	378	401	386	495	3242	6443
White	484	118	395	280	136	339	389	336	472	2610	5959
Forward	427	100	323	209	122	286	310	259	408	2444	4963
Par	5	3	4	4	3	4	4	4	5	36	72

Below opposite: **A view of the seventeenth hole, looking over the green and back along the fairway. Valhalla includes such subtleties as the ridge that adds complexity to the fourth green (see page 173).**

The tenth hole is a double dogleg—left, then right—to a shallow, irregular green having a bunker on its right front. Trees line the left, and mounds line the right, of this hole. Hole number eleven is a par three; its green has trees at left, right and behind, a bunker at right rear, and a large crescent bunker all along its front. The twelfth hole is a dogleg right with trees right and left, and mounding at the left end of the fairway that will force your shot down the long green approach to the right. The green is set in a cul-de-sac of mounds, and has a bunker on its exposed right front. This is a targeting challenge.

Hole number thirteen is a dogleg left with a long carry from the back tees to the short, broad fairway. Beyond the mounds to the right is the beautiful terraced waterfall that comes into play on the eighteenth hole. Mounds to the left, and trees and a bunker to the right, make a broad staging ground for the green approach shot, which must carry over Floyds Fork to an island green surrounded by a stone wall that fronts on the water. It's an exciting test of accuracy. The back tee of hole number fourteen—a par three—occupies the same island as the aforesaid green, and from here, it's a water carry to a green that nestles into a grove of trees. Occupying a large part of the exposed face of the green is a bunker.

Golfers at hole number fifteen tee off with Floyds Fork to the right of the tees, and the stream meanders on along the right side of the slender fairway. On the left of the fairway, and to the left and rear of the green, is a forest, and many golfers will attempt a carry down a segment of the stream to the green, as the water impinges on the green approach from the right. The sixteenth plays back in the opposite direction, with a carry over Floyds Fork from the back tee. This is a rather tricky carry, as the blue and white tees are elevated to the left, and mounds and trees to the right help to form a 'gunsight' for the shot to the fairway. Trees and a stream along the right of the fairway further define this hole, and the green will test your putting skills.

The seventeenth hole has a long carry from the back tees, and its undulating fairway will be a challenge. The inner tees have a challenge in the bunker that lies to the left of the landing spot, as overflights could find the sand here. A rock wall surrounds the green on three sides, and a mound at right rear, plus bunkering at left front, make this green a challenge.

The eighteenth hole has a split fairway, and employs a diversity of 'challenge techniques' similar to that encountered at hole number seven. Golfers here tee off across Floyds Fork to a fairway that has heavy mounding all along its left. To the right, Floyds Fork widens to become a spectacular, and very distracting, tiered waterfall that leads to the right of the green approach. Golfers at the landing spot have their choice: at the green approach, the fairway forks left and right around a large bunker that heads into the center of the green. The left fork is landlocked, but leads to a less advantageous approach than does the right fork, which is reachable by a carry over the waterfall. The green is a broad, shallow 'vee.' Behind are mounds, and in front, a long, narrow bunker. With multiple tiers, this green is a thinking man's challenge, and a truly great summation to an outstanding eighteen holes of golf.

Wabeek Country Club

Bloomfield Hills, Michigan USA

J ack Nicklaus cooperated with Pete Dye in the designing of the Wabeek Golf Course. This beautiful layout rambles over 150 acres, and though, at 6600 yards from the championship tees, it is not a long course, it provides a superb test of golf. Elevated greens and an abundance of water hazards, lakes and trees combine to make this not only a beautiful, but also a memorable, course.

Wabeek was the brainchild of a joint venture involving Chrysler Realty Corporation and Del E Webb, Inc, and was conceived as a residential, golf-oriented, resort community. The first construction on the facility began in 1974, along with the Country Club, which was restricted to use by Wabeek residents. In April 1983 the membership voted to allow non-residents to become members.

Wabeek is now a private, non-profit organization wholly owned by members holding regular stock. The club is maturing into one of the area's most prestigious clubs, and has a broad ethnic base that gives it a cosmopolitan ambience.

The Wabeek Clubhouse is a handsome, contemporary building that provides spectacular, sweeping views of the course. Cocktails in the Grille or a fine lunch or dinner in the Main Salon are regular amenities, and combine with dinner-dances, informal buffets and casual cookouts to grant the Clubhouse a warmly social atmosphere.

Below: **The thirteenth green at the Wabeek course, a Pete Dye-Jack Nicklaus collaboration.** *At right:* **The sixteenth green, with the seventeenth tees to its left and the seventeenth fairway in the background.**

Tennis thrives at Wabeek, with full facilities and participation in lively interclub competition. Swimming facilities include a beautiful, Olympic-size free-form pool, a spacious lounge and other amenities to make the pool area a natural meeting place for groups of all ages. An ongoing training/teaching program is conducted throughout the Memorial Day to Labor Day season.

The Golf Course at Wabeek includes such amenities as a driving range and lesson area, a wide putting green, and a separate chipping/bunker practice area. An underground storage facility for the club-owned golf cart fleet has recently been completed, and a wide range of golfing activities, numerous tournaments and club-sponsored groups add to the richness of the experience of golfing at Wabeek. Wabeek is a member of the Golf Association of Michigan, and is staffed by PGA professionals.

The following is a hole-by-hole description of this fine Pete Dye/Jack Nicklaus-designed course. The first hole is a dogleg left, and plays away from the clubhouse. A thicket can be seen over to the left, but you'd best maintain your concentration here, as the best is yet to come. Hole number two is a severe dogleg right in form, and its broad fairway leads to a small and irregular green.

The third hole is a par three, and plays

These pages: **A wide-open vista at Wabeek. The change-of-season beauty seen here is only part of the pleasure of playing this exciting, challenging course.**

straightaway to a deep, but narrow, green—it's a real test of accuracy. Hole number four has greenery all along its left, and the green itself will test your putting skill. The fifth hole is a long par four, with a serpentine fairway and a challenging green. Distinctly different tee approaches make this one play a number of intriguing ways.

Hole number six is straightaway, with verdure on its right-hand side. It's a good warm-up for the seventh hole, which is one of the toughest tests of golf in Michigan. A dogleg left, this one features a 'gunsight' composed of trees right and left, making the tee shot a matter of extra concentration. Just after the trees, and all the way to the green approach, a lake lies just off the fairway to the left. It's a hole that will challenge you as few others will.

The eighth hole is a par three, and tests your accuracy and sense of distance with a small, slippery, green. Hole number nine is a dogleg right that plays back toward the clubhouse. Varying tee positions allow a great variety of play at this hole.

Hole number ten plays away from the clubhouse, with a lake all along its right side. The small green is a real challenge, and the water's closeness is a distraction, and a challenge in itself. The eleventh hole features a carry over water from the tees, and its dogleg configuration adds drama to this hole. Hole number twelve is a dogleg left, with water along its left side, and a subtle green.

The thirteenth hole is a par three. Tee shots must carry over the edge of a lake to the right,

At right: **Striking vistas abound, and an excellent upkeep program ensures top-knotch conditions for play at Wabeek. Note the naturalness of this course.**

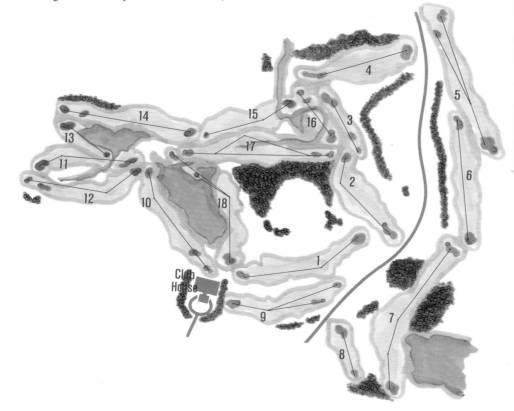

Hole	1	2	3	4	5	6	7	8	9	Out	
Blue	480	326	189	362	427	377	579	162	378	3280	
White	452	298	155	347	366	357	576	157	318	3026	
Red	412	275	136	279	302	338	502	142	287	2673	
Par	5	4	3	4	4	4	5	3	4	36	
Hole	10	11	12	13	14	15	16	17	18	In	Total
Blue	373	328	376	209	391	344	181	505	437	3144	6426
White	356	307	363	153	368	333	155	480	378	2893	5919
Red	309	270	306	132	338	222	116	453	270	2516	5189
Par	4	4	4	3	4	4	3	5	4	35	71

These pages: An elegant composition in green. Wabeek Country Club is known as one of the finest facilities in the region. Its classic proportions and verdant setting combine to provide an extraordinary test of golf.

and the wide, shallow green is hard to hold on to. Hole number fourteen has a serpentine fairway with water on its right and a green that will challenge your putting ability. The fifteenth hole has a stream across its green approach, and water also on the right of the green. Precision is the key here.

The sixteenth hole is a very distracting and challenging par three, with the bend of a stream providing lots of water between the tees and the green. Shots to the right of the green will find water, as will shortfalls in almost any direction here. The seventeenth hole provides an interesting variant, with its split fairway in the Scottish manner. Golfers at the tees can choose to go straight ahead to the green, or to make a water carry to the right—over the wide branch of a stream—for a greater challenge.

The eighteenth hole shares the toughness honors on this course with hole number seven. Golfers at the tees face an oblique water carry to the fairway, which features, as an approach to the green, another water carry. The green will test your putting skills; it's a great finish to a very fine eighteen hole test of golf.

Above: **The sixteenth's inner tee and green (in the distance).** *At right:* **As is evident here, this course harmonizes with its natural surroundings.** *Below:* **The second green, with the seventeenth tees to its left.**

These pages: **A view of several lake holes at Wabeek. A combination of natural and man-made hazards make this course an exceptional and satisfying challenge.**

INDEX

Photo Credits

All-Sport: 8
John Briggs via Glen Abbey Golf Club: 72-73, 81 (bottom)
© Barbara Broske via Glen Abbey Golf Club: 74-75
© Bill Frantz via Americana Lake Geneva Resort: 18
Golf Photography International: 107 (bottom), 108, 109, 110-111
© John Knight: 4-5, 20-21, 22-23, 25, 26-27
Ralph Moore via The Country Club of Castle Pines: 48 (both), 49

(top), 51 (top)
© Brian Morgan Golf Photography: 1, 7, 38, 39, 40-41 (both), 42-43, 44 (top), 45, 46 (both), 54 (bottom), 56 (top), 66-67, 68, 82 (bottom), 84-85, 86, 87, 102, 107 (top left), 148 (both), 149 (all), 150 (all), 151, 158-159, 159 (top), 160, 172, 173, 176
© Jim Moriarty via The Country Club of Castle Pines: 49 (bottom), 50-51
© Fred Mullane via Sea Pines Plantation Company, Inc: 98-99
Pete Park via Park Meadows Country Club: 136
© Carl Scofield: 2-3, 28 (both), 29, 30, 31, 32 (both), 33 (both), 34, 35, 36-37, 192
© Michael Tenney via The Melrose Club: 120, 121, 123 (both)
Texas Tourist Development Agency: 103, 104, 105
Frank Zullo via Desert Highlands Development Company: 54 (top), 58 (top)

Below: **A greenward view of Harbour Town Golf Links, with scenic vistas all around, and great golf at hand.** *Overleaf:* **Set in vastly different surroundings. a green at Breckenridge.**